STATISTS
SAVING
ONE

*(Also Available
in Hardcover)*

STATISTS
SAVING
ONE

THE MALIGNANT SOPHISTRY
OF RIGHTS REMOVAL
BY THE FAR LEFT

J. BARTHOLOMEW WALKER

Quadrakoff Publications Group, LLC
Wilmington, Delaware
USA

They have been circulating among us
for quite some time,
relying upon the fact that few knew this.

That just changed...

.

Contents

Chapter 1

Rights

Rights; what are they?

Often used interchangeably; rights, privileges, permits, licenses, etc.; are "seeming synonyms;" often used to describe the allowance of a given behavior, without the imposition of negative consequences by society. But what; if anything; is it that is *peculiar* about "rights?"

Rights; unlike the aforementioned "pseudo-synonyms," are not *granted* to man by man; but rather come with the package—meaning endowed to man by its or our Creator. To have rights, one need only to be born.

And irrespective of whether or not these rights are recognized, they nevertheless exist. The

Creator has endowed "certain" rights to His Creation; and He has done so for "certain" reasons.
    Genesis 1:28 (KJV) tells us:

> *"And God blessed them,*
> *and God said unto them,*
> *Be fruitful, and multiply,*
> *and replenish the earth,*
> *and subdue it:*
>
> *and have dominion over the*
> *fish of the sea,*
> *and over the fowl of the air,*
> *and over every living thing*
> *that moveth upon the earth."*[1.1]

    "The actual word translated as "replenish" is:

> "4390 mâlê'; or mâlâ' (Esth. 7:5),; a prim. root, to *fill* or (intrans.) *be full* of, in a wide application (lit. and fig.)..."[1A] [It is unclear as to why Esther is referenced here, as mâlê' in Esther 7:5 is translated as "presume" in the KJV.[1A]]

"The actual word translated as "subdue" is:

> "3533 kâbash; a prim. root;
> to *tread* down; hence neg.
> to *disregard*; pos. to
> *conquer*, *subjugate*,
> *violate*: - bring into
> bondage, force, keep
> under, subdue, bring into
> subjection.[1B] A slight
> variant of this is seen in
> current English
> vernacular, although it is
> spelled *kibosh*.

"The actual word translated as "dominion" is:

> "7287 râdâh; to *tread*
> down, i.e. *subjugate*; spec.
> to *crumble* of: - (come to
> make to) have dominion,
> prevail against, reign,
> (bear, make to) rule, (-r,
> over), take."[1C]

"There are two points contained here in Genesis 1:28 worthy of "considerable consideration:"

"*Firstly*; it is clear that it is God's will that man have dominion over the earth. God is establishing and instructing His wishes with regard to man's relationship to the earth, *and* all the life forms upon the earth. He told man to "subdue it: and have dominion." Thus this refers to both the earth itself, "subdue *it*; as well as to "have dominion" over all the other various life forms—"over every living thing that moveth upon the earth..."[1.2] [excerpt from: "*Shâmar to Sharia*" Reprinted by Permission]

Thus it seems clear; that in furtherance of the instructions contained here in Genesis 1:28, man would need to maintain a certain level of *individual* authority, with respect to the activities that his Creator both *instructed* and *designed* man to undertake.

The "Declaration of Independence" tells us:

> "*We hold these truths to be self-evident,*
> *that all men are created equal, that*
> *they are endowed by their Creator with*
> *certain unalienable Rights, that among*
> *these are Life, Liberty and*
> *the pursuit of Happiness.*
>
> *That to secure these rights,*
> *Governments are instituted among*
> *Men, deriving their just Powers from*
> *the consent of the governed...*"[1.3]

The first noteworthy area for disagreement; is the use of the term: "certain." This is often interpreted as a synonym for "particular" or "these particular;" as in: "certain types of individuals are. . ." However; a more compelling argument for the use of "certain" would be as used in the phrase: "the existence of these rights is a certainty"— opinions of any "experts" notwithstanding. Here the existence of these rights is not subject to any debate, as *it* and *they* are a certainty.

The next noteworthy area for disagreement; is the use of term: "unalienable." Man cannot be separated from his rights; i.e.; "unable to be alienated from." This *certain* existence of these rights, and the inability for any person or persons to *separate* man from his rights, is entirely different than the lawful *suppression* of the *expression* of these rights.

It also must be noted that the use of "among these;" indicates that "Life, Liberty, and Pursuit of Happiness" represent by no means an exhaustive list; but rather merely represent a *subset* of the much larger set of rights; with these same arguably to either already be known, or to be delineated at another time.

And why is government "instituted;" i.e.; what is the purpose of government? We are told here; "That to secure these rights, Governments are instituted among Men." Thus; government's purpose is not to *create*, (as it cannot), or *institute* rights; but rather "to secure" these same rights that existed long before this particular government, or any other government even existed. Thus these rights predate the establishment of any government; or in a sense with respect to any government, represent a "pre-existing condition."

There is also another generally glossed over distinction being made here: "deriving their just Powers from the consent of the governed..." This statement is concerned not with the powers of government; but rather only the *just* powers of government. This one simple adjective, lets all know that unless any given power is derived "from the consent of the governed;" whatever else this or these may represent; these are not *just* powers. Thus any and all powers other than those derived from the "consent of the governed;" are *ultra-vires*, or "without authority," or "beyond the powers" of said government.

If it can be so stipulated that "just" here is a binary; meaning that something is either *just* or *unjust*, irrespective of the perceived magnitude or the degree of the "justice;" then any powers not derived "from the consent of the governed" are by definition *unjust*. Precisely how greatly unjust said *ultra-vires* powers may in fact be, although relevant to many other considerations; is *irrelevant* with respect to the binary determination of whether or not any given power is to be considered a *just* power. If it is derived from the consent of the governed, then it is *just*; if it is not, then it is *unjust*.

A word here about "consent." It must be asked: Precisely what is the difference between "consent," and "informed consent?" And further; can there be any such thing as "uninformed consent?" If consent is based upon falsehood, the same is based upon that which merely appears or is believed to be so; but is actually based upon that which is not. Thus any consent based upon clear and deliberate falsehood, as opposed to genuine error; automatically becomes null and void. This will not in any way guarantee any change in a law or policy based upon said deception; but does change any purported "*just* power" to an "*unjust* power."

In a sense, "That to secure these rights, governments are instituted among men;" represents *specialization*. Government is instituted to protect the rights of society, so that each individual can spend his time and efforts elsewhere. Unfortunately; if there is a hen house, sooner or later there will be a fox.

An *Emmanic Principle* states:

> "*If one wants to find a thief, simply find something of perceived value and wait. Sooner or later the thief will show up.*"[*.4]—Emma B. Quadrakoff

The Fifth, (and later the Fourteenth with regard to the states), amendments; tell us how important these rights are with respect to any *denial* of these rights stating: "nor be deprived of life, liberty, or property, without due process of law."[1.5]

Thus absent the "due process of law," or "informed consent;" each individual's rights must be maintained, and any action that in any way interferes with any individual's rights without due process of law is meaningless with respect to *just* power. This is not to say that *unjust* power does not exist, but rather that it is not consistent with the "consent of the governed" requirement, and thus is *ultra-vires*.

Are there are any possible limits to an individual's rights, or perhaps better phrased: Are there any possible limits to the *exercise* of an individual's rights? The answer of course is most certainly. How is it that any limits to the exercise of an individual's rights can be determined? The answer is quite simple and unique:

> *"The only just criterion for limiting the expression of an individual's rights; is if said expression can reasonably be expected to interfere with the expression of another individual's rights."*[1.6]—Emma B. Quadrakoff

James Madison is credited with having said:

> *"Liberty may be endangered by the abuse of liberty, but also by the abuse of power."*[1.7]—James Madison

The first part is correctly seen with the "fire in a crowded theatre" limitations on free speech, otherwise guaranteed by the 1st Amendment. Here the exercise of free speech by yelling fire in a crowded theatre; is outweighed by the rights of "life" of those individuals in the theatre—assuming of course that there is no fire.

The test is not that any given expression of rights *could* interfere, *might* interfere, is *possible* to interfere; but rather that it is reasonably determined that it *will* interfere with the rights of another. Neither is the test concerned with whether or not the expression is liked agreed with, or even "nice." The 1st Amendment would not be necessary for expression that everyone liked, or that or those with which one, many, or all agreed.

Any subsequent judicial diminutions notwithstanding; the fact remains that interference with another's rights must be both *clear* and *present* in order to justify interference with the rights of the active party. Banning the purchase or possession of pyrotechnic devices, (common fireworks), because they might be used by someone, at some time, for some illegal purpose, that may harm someone somewhere; fails to meet this test. Fireworks are not explosive devices that are designed to "kill people and break things;" but rather are for expression and enjoyment. The same can be said for the banning the possession or carrying of firearms by law abiding citizens. However the same test cannot be applied for those who have already lawfully been proven to be a menace to society.

The meaning of the second part of Madison's quote: "*but also by the abuse of power*," is clear to any being capable of rational thought.

Chapter 2

The Sophists

The title of this tome is: "*Statists Saving One.*" An alternative title could be: "*Even if it Saves Just One,*" as often this; with some noun added after the word "one;" is proffered as sufficient reason for depriving a citizen or class of citizens of their God given unalienable rights.

The seemingly most common usage, being the insertion of the word "life," so that it reads: "statists saving one life;" more commonly stated as: "even if it saves just one life." And it is often followed by: "it is worth it to..." This is often proffered as justification for depriving lawful citizens of their 2nd Amendment rights to some incalculable, and non-objective degree. The inclusion of the word "if" here should not be overlooked.

But it would be both interesting and fair to rephrase this statement as an "equationoid," in order to try and determine if this position has any degree of validity:

If It Saves Just One Life ≥ |Certain Deprivation of Constitutional Rights|

Here it is being stated that the positive magnitude of the "value" of possibly saving one life; is *greater* than or *equal* to; (here illustrated by the symbol ≥); the "absolute value" of the negative magnitude of the value of the amount of harm caused by the deprivation of the exercise of constitutional rights.

"Absolute value" must be used here, as any said deprivation of rights is harmful to an individual, and thus represents a negative number. Thus; since any small positive number, or even zero, is always greater than a negative; the actual magnitude, or distance from zero on a number line, is necessary for comparison. [This is similar to the use of the Kelvin scale for temperature, where the value must *never* be a negative number for gas calculations such as: $PV=nRT$.]

For example: Hypothetically; if the value for saving one life was say +10; no matter what the negative value of the willful deprivation of constitutional rights, the equation would hold; as a positive number is always greater than any negative number. So the negative value of the willful deprivation of constitutional rights would be useless, and thus its absolute value or actual *magnitude* must be utilized.

This "equationoid," represents the "logic" generally utilized to justify a position that outlaws certain types of weapons or weapon magazines deemed by some as unnecessary for actions such as: "to kill ahh deeeahhh." These types of statements are often made as though the 2nd Amendment was somehow designed exclusively for use against quadrupeds.

If the complete left side of the "equation;" the "If it saves just one life," is assigned a variable say x; the true value of x is actually determined by the combination or product of two things: First would be the *value* of that one human life. The second would be the *probability* as expressed by the "if." The product of multiplying the value by the probability would determine the value of x. This is similar to *expected value* in games of chance—how much is the prize, and what is the probability or likelihood of winning it.

However with regard to the use of this for the deprivation of say 2nd Amendment rights; there are at a minimum two other concerns:

First; there is the requirement that there exists a *cause-effect* relationship between the availability of that which is to be banned, and the subsequent unjustified loss of human life. Meaning; will the rights depriving banning of certain weapons actually save a life or lives; or will it merely cause the criminal to simply ignore the ban; or find a less expensive and thus more efficient means? The existence of a weapon itself does not represent any type of *cause*, but is merely a *means*. If the black market cost of a banned weapon increases enough, high explosives may then become *relatively* inexpensive.

The second concern; is the *effect* that the rights depriving banning of types of weapons could have on their lawful use as self-defensive tools. The use of a shotgun; (assuming these are not also banned); requires that the target be at much closer range than with a rifle. A handgun is a weapon of last defense/resort, (excluding rocks, sticks, and fists); and thus the target generally needs to be even closer. Likewise; the banning of "high capacity" magazines, might require the victim to have the criminal "wait while I reload." Overall gun related deaths could actually increase—irrespective of any lack of reporting of the same.

But back to the "validity" of the "equation." If this "logic" is sound; then it should be applicable to other matters.

Here again is the "equation:"

$$\text{If It Saves Just One Life} \geq |\text{Certain Deprivation of Constitutional Rights}|$$

There is little doubt that more people are killed in automobile related accidents, than are killed by gun violence. So here, instead of applying this "equation" to the rights depriving banning of 2nd Amendments rights; what happens if this "equation" were to be applied to automobiles?

According to this same "equation," but here with "it" referring to the banning of automobiles that "saves just one life;" if this equation were valid; i.e.; using the same "logic;" then the rights depriving banning of automobiles would certainly be worth it.

"Whoa—wait a minute! You can't ban automobiles!" The correct response of course would be the question: "Why not?" If this purported "equation" holds; then many more lives would be saved by the rights depriving banning of automobiles, than would ever be saved by rights depriving banning of certain 2nd Amendment rights.

The answer of course lies in the actual *value* of the |Certain Deprivation of Constitutional Rights| part of the equation. Those who would proffer rights depriving banning of weapons, do not see the magnitude of value of the 2nd Amendment infringements as being anywhere near the magnitude of the value of the rights depriving infringements that would be caused by the banning of automobiles. This is despite the fact that many more lives would be saved.

Those who proffer the rights depriving banning of anything, therefore have an "analog" view of rights; when rights are in fact a *binary*. They believe that it is *they* who determine for *all*, the values of these "certain unalienable Rights, that among these are Life, Liberty and the pursuit of Happiness." Since it is *their* view; that unlike 2nd Amendment rights; the harm caused by banning automobiles would be so great, that the loss of thousands of lives on an annual basis is a relatively small price to pay, compared to the abolishment of automobiles.

But according to those very Founding Documents which authorize the very existence of the very authority that those who wish the banning of otherwise constitutionally guaranteed rights proffer; the very purpose and function of government is *"to secure these rights,"* as *"Governments are instituted among Men, deriving their just Powers from the consent of the governed..."*

Government by design; is supposed to protect these rights on a binary basis, and not to determine the value of various rights on behalf of those from whom their "powers" are derived. And even if this were so, clearly the 2nd Amendment is of much more value than all others with the exception of the 1st—as this is precisely why it is the second, and not the tenth.

Once again here is the "equation:"

$$\text{If It Saves Just One Life} \geq |\text{Certain Deprivation of Constitutional Rights}|$$

It would be interesting to try and apply this "equation" to the military.

It is more than arguable to state that the main purpose of the military is to protect the rights of citizens; most especially life and liberty. Thus this "equation" falls completely apart if an attempt is made to apply this to the military. The military is willing to lose countless numbers of lives in order to protect the rights of citizens.

So here the "equation" kind of "flips" with the military. In fact with regard to the *military*, this "equation" now becomes:

$$|\text{Certain Deprivation of Constitutional Rights}| \geq$$
The Loss of Countless Numbers of Lives

How can this be? $2 + 2 = 4$ works with money, bananas, electrons, and everything else known in the universe. It is much more reliable than even Geometry; as there is that pesky Euclidian vs. Non-Euclidian, (non-curved vs. curved universe), issue.

But here it seems that this equation represents an *absolute* when proffered for 2nd Amendment and many other rights deprivations; *not applicable* with respect to utilizing automobiles for freedom of movement, and *reverses* itself with respect to the military. Thus this represents no equation or law at all. It merely represents a feeble attempt to justify the unjustifiable.

Karl Popper is reputed to have stated:

> "*A theory that explains everything,
> explains nothing.*"[2.1]

This is presented here as an *absolute* in that: "A theory that..." in fact reasonably means "Any and all theory(ies) that..." Might it also be the case, that at least with respect to the subject matter at hand; that a modified reversal may also be true?

Specifically: "A theory, (or purported law), that explains *nothing*; can explain *everything*."

If simply for the purpose of discussion, it is stipulated that this *could* be so; then the first; and likely the most common definition of a theory that explains nothing, is that it is merely idiocy—thus the "explanation of everything" is necessarily that the "profferer" of the same is merely an idiot—Voila!

Stated differently: "That theory you are purporting which explains nothing, is idiocy; and of no possible use. Who needs a theory that explains nothing?"

However it must be remembered that the word "idiot," generally means "doesn't know," or "unknown." This is seen in words such as *idiopathic*; meaning a disease with an "unknown cause."

It may in fact be the case that one who proffers that a theory or law that explains nothing, somehow explains everything; is that the "profferer" of this proffering is simply an idiot.

However; it may also be that said theory or law explains everything in another way. The same being, that this theory or law that explains nothing; does in fact explain everything; but the true "everything" is hidden.

Meaning, that the observer fails to grasp the true meaning; and thus here it is the observer who is the true idiot, or "doesn't know." This is often because the *scruples* of the observer. preclude the observer from true and correct observation.

Popper is also reputed to have said:

The Sophists

*"Those who promise us
paradise on earth
never produced anything but a hell."*[2.2]

Chapter 3

The Statists

The founding fathers never promised paradise on earth—Far from it. James Madison wrote:

> "If men were angels, no government would be necessary. If angels were to govern men, neither external nor internal controls on government would be necessary.
>
> In framing a government which is to be administered by men over men, the great difficulty lies in this: you must first enable the government to control the governed; and in the next place oblige it to control itself."[3.1]

Here is seen Madison's incredibly clear understanding of what will inevitably happen with any government. The use of the terms "enable" and "oblige" should not be overlooked. Enable essentially represents the transfer of ability from one, (or the many); to that which does not have said ability; in order to permit the same to have such ability. The use of "oblige" is not to be confused with "may," "might," "I hope," or "perhaps." The use of "oblige" refers to an obligation or debt, with the same here being for "it" to control "itself."

Scientist and author David Brin is attributed with having stated:

> *"It is said that power corrupts, but*
> *actually it's more true that power*
> *attracts the corruptible.*
> *The sane are usually attracted by*
> *other things than power."*[3.2]

The use of "more true" here represents a *degree* of truth, rather than truth vs. falsehood. Here Brin admits that it is "true" that power does in fact corrupt, but it is "more true;" (true vs. more true, as opposed to false vs. true); that "power attracts the corruptible."

It should be asked precisely how the truly "un-corruptible" could possibly be corrupted? Thus in the case of power "corrupting," it necessarily follows that this cannot apply to anyone who is truly un-corruptible—and there have been some in government to whom this applies. Thus because of this, it seems that "power corrupts" is "less true" than "power attracts the corruptible."

Power can only corrupt he who is corruptible; and thus power *attracts* those who are corruptible. Although it does not necessarily follow that power *repels* those who are un-corruptible, it can be reasonably inferred that at a minimum, power itself does not attract them.

This leads to the "conclusion" of the quote: "The sane are usually attracted by other things than power." The word "sane" is derived from the Latin *sanus*; which means healthy in the *general* sense. Often sane or sanity is used synonymously with *mental* health, but sanitary, sanitation, etc., are also derived from *sanus*. There is a tacit admission here that only those who are *not* attracted to power are in fact *sanus* or healthy. Thus if one is attracted to power, there then must necessarily be some degree of foundational "unhealthyness"—else no such attraction could or would exist.

Words mean things; and thus it may in fact be the case that the ""sane" are *never* attracted by power. They only sometimes *appear* to be attracted by or to the power—with George Washington arguable being a prime example. If it is something other than power that is the desired end result, but the acquisition of some governmental power is the necessary prerequisite, (tautology noted), in order to achieve these ends; it is the *ends* that provide the attraction, with the power acquisition merely being a "necessary evil." Thus here, the *ends* represent the "other things than power," which provides the attraction.

In fact, the acquisition of power may in fact be considered as abhorrent to the sane. However; sometimes the desire to achieve the ends is so great, that said desire outweighs whatever degree of repulsion to the acquisition of power is present. When this "desire" is overwhelming among the "sane;" i.e.; those who are attracted to things "other than power;" this can often be what is called a *talanton*. And a true talanton is always accompanied by some level of *dunamis*, or *supernatural* power. [See the monograph: "*Donald Trump Candidacy According to Matthew*?" for an explanation of this process.]

Brin's statement: "power attracts the corruptible," represents another, but more general way of stating the previously cited Emmanic principle: "If one wants to find a thief, simply find something of perceived value and wait. Sooner or later the thief will show up."

This leads to making significant distinctions between the two groups that generally promote restrictions on individual liberties, but usually are grouped into one. Irrespective of the accuracy of the term with respect to its *origins*; today, it is those who are considered *liberals* who are generally associated with suppression, infringement, and interference with individual's rights; for what they believe, or claim to believe, constitutes the "greater good."

Although the term "progressive" is often proffered as a synonym for "liberal," this is not so:

"It must be remembered that progressivism, (in the political context); is not a political ideology; but rather is a tactic or strategy, depending upon its use. To characterize one's self as a "progressive" politically, merely means that one believes in placing the frog in a pot of cold water and placing the pot on the stove; rather than placing the frog in boiling water; because the frog then could and likely would simply jump out.

The enemy is and has been an expert at this type of progressivism. In fact it can be reasonably argued that he (it) invented it."[3.3] [Excerpt from: "Shâmar to Sharia" Reprinted by permission]

James Madison said:

"I believe there are more instances of the abridgement of freedom of the people by gradual and silent encroachments by those in power than by violent and sudden usurpations."[3.4]

During the "Cuban Missile Crisis," Fidel Castro is reputed to have stated that the United States tolerating nuclear weapons in Cuba was (paraphrased): "Like a man forced to live with a cow—He doesn't like it, but he'll get used to it."

Progressivism, (political), can be utilized by the right or the left. It merely represents the exploitation of scruples, and the calculated abuse of "mental homeostasis."

But under the umbrella of "liberals," or "liberalism;" (as used today); there are actually two separate and distinct groups:

True *liberals* believe very much in what they, promulgate. They are truly concerned with the welfare of citizens, and they believe in policies that will benefit the same—at least in their view. There are neither nefarious purposes, nor any intellectual dishonesty. Their objective is to improve the quality of life (and longevity), for as many people as possible.

Whether as a practical matter, the purported policies of true liberals can possibly be meaningfully sustained, is a subject of great debate. Nevertheless; their motives are in no way selfish or self-centered; in fact the opposite is true.

This is the subject of a quote which may or may not be from Winston Churchill:

> *"If you're not a liberal when you're 25,*
> *you have no heart.*
> *If you're not a conservative*
> *by the time you're 35,*
> *you have no brain."*[3.5]

Arguably; this quote contrasts the *emotional* desires of true liberalism, with the *practicality* of the same. Conservatives and true liberals can often agree on the *ends*; but vastly disagree on the *means*. Giving a hungry person a fish is kind; but to conservatives, teaching him how to fish seems to be a better long term solution. It is not that conservatives object to the temporary giving of the fish; but rather they object to *not* teaching him how to fish.

True liberals believe in the dignity of man; and promulgate policies in furtherance of this belief.

Statists; the other group usually, and often erroneously grouped under the "liberal" umbrella; are another matter. It is because of agreements with liberal *policy*, that they are usually grouped under this liberal umbrella; but their *motivations*, *purposes* and *beliefs* are entirely different—arguably antithetical—to true liberalism.

As distasteful, disgusting, and unbelievable, (for now), this may be; the unavoidable, logical, necessary, and predictable end product of statism is often eugenics. This will be addressed later.

Precisely what is a "statist;" and/or what is "statism?"

Merriam Webster defines a *statist* as:

> "an advocate of statism."[3.6]

This of course provides little illumination.
Merriam Webster defines *statism* as:

> "concentration of economic controls and planning in the hands of a highly centralized government often extending to government ownership of industry."[3.7]

If the two are combined, it is easy to see that a statist is one who is "an advocate of concentration of economic controls and planning in the hands of a highly centralized government often extending to government ownership of industry."

It must be asked, as to precisely *why* one would be a statist? These definitions provide no insight as to what would make one believe in, or be an "advocate" of statism; i.e.; *why* is one a statist?

If it can be so stipulated, (for now), that a statist is such not because he or she is in favor of less production and wealth; but rather believes that the "concentration of economic controls and planning in the hands of a highly centralized government often extending to government ownership of industry;" i.e.; *statism*; is a *better* system; it then becomes obvious *why* statists are statists. [It will be seen later however, that this stipulation is not warranted.]

So the question becomes not why one is a *statist*, (as that is simply because one believes in statism); but rather why does one believe that *statism* represents a better system? Why does one believe that a "highly centralized government" is better at "economic controls and planning" and even "industry;" than are free market forces? Surely experience shows us that the government is considered by most to be the most *inefficient* means of getting anything done—as the eight hundred dollar toilets, (in 1980's dollars), did not manifest all that long ago.

According to Conservapedia:

> "A statist government treats its political sovereignty as a platform for

*moral sovereignty. In other words, as
ultimate sovereign, the state is
therefore not subject to God the Bible
natural law, or any other religion or
ethical system. A statist government
need not be accountable to its own
citizens.*"[3.8]

Thus statism does not seem to be based upon
any notion that government is capable of any
higher degrees of efficiency; but rather, it is based
upon a much deeper disagreement with
Judeo/Christian concepts.

"If there is any legitimate use for the
'separation of church and state' rule;
this should be utilized to prevent the
government from religious
proselytizing, not to be used to justify
1st Amendment restrictions on US
citizens; simply because of a money
trail purportedly providing the
government with jurisdiction—i.e.; the
authority but not the *right*.

"To the extent that God and His
rules for behavior can either be
removed, made inaccessible, or
"uncool;" then *His* rules are necessarily
then supplanted by *man's* rules, which
over millennia simply did not work.
Clearly one cannot *shâmar* what one
has never read or understood. This is
not an unintended consequence, but

rather the main objective of those who are making access to God's word as difficult as possible.

"The inevitable result of this, is a government that can, (now must), become ever increasingly involved with regulating what H. Sapiens *can* do, because what H. Sapiens *will* do has changed so dramatically. This change is the direct result of deliberately and with malice making God's rules as inaccessible as possible..."[3.9] [Excerpt from" *"Shâmar to Sharia"* Reprinted by permission]

At least the statists are honest, in the sense that they openly proclaim that it is man via the *collective* that is the ultimate authority—but of course that proclamation in no way makes it in any way true.

As sophomoric as this may seem, it must always be remembered that there is that which is, and there is that which is not. That which is: exists both as an *actuality*; and also a *reality* to the extent that it is accurately perceived. That which is not, can exist as a *reality* only, having no basis in actuality.

The reality of a desert *mirage* is water. But the actuality of the mirage, (if it is a mirage), does not include any water. If the reality of the presence of water is also an actuality; then this would not and could not be a mirage by definition.

That which creates, creates. That which does not create or cannot create; does not create and cannot create. If that which does not or cannot create, appears to create; this represents at best, merely a mirage. This resultant *quasi-reality*, is that that which does not create and cannot create; yet somehow nevertheless created. But by definition that which does not or cannot create, did not create. There may sometimes exist a *reality* of a creation being the result of that which does not or cannot create; but there can be no *actuality* of any creation being the result of that which does not or cannot create.

That which creates, (creator); necessarily creates in a manner consistent with that which is of the creator. The creator cannot create in any other manner.

Adam had no knowledge of evil. That which brought Adam into existence; (although not technically *created* but *formed*); did not include any possibility of the inclusion of any evil. Thus Adam could have had no "first hand" knowledge of evil; as in all possible subsets of the creator, there was no possibility of the inclusion of evil in any of them.

The creator had the "knowledge" of evil; but did not contain the evil itself. Evil, and even so much as the *knowledge* of evil, had to be *brought* to Adam—and it was. The *knowledge* of evil was possessed by the creator, but the creator contained no evil. Thus the creator had to provide the knowledge of evil by permitting the evil, and thus the *knowledge* of evil, to come to Adam. Had the

31

creator attempted to merely explain evil to Adam, likely Adam could not possibly have understood.

Often the antonyms of "good" are considered to be both *evil* and *bad*. However; distinctions must be made between evil and bad. If it can be so stipulated; that *evil* means against God's will; thereby the reference being God's *will*, irrespective of the "quality" of the act itself; and if it can be further stipulated that *bad* or *wicked* refers to that very "quality" of the act itself, irrespective of whether or not it is consistent with God's will; things can become a bit interesting.

The Crucifixion was clearly a *bad* or *wicked* act. However; it was not an *evil* act, as this was the very purpose for which Jesus was born—according to Christianity.

Even if one is not a Christian, and considers this a mere myth; the distinction still holds, even if only hypothetically. Likewise; if Jesus had come to a different decision at Gethsemane, and decided *not* to "go through with it;" this would have been good in the sense that the horrors would have been avoided; but at the same time would have been *evil*, as it was God's will that He did "go through with it." Thus; this would also likely then have been a "sin."

Given this understanding; it must be asked precisely how God could possibly have any *evil* within him? How could God simultaneously have the same thing be both *consistent* with His will, and at the same time be *inconsistent* with; i.e.; *against*; His will?

As an aside, when Jesus was asked about the date of the "end times," He refused to provide the same; responding in a manner generally translated as: "only the Father knows." It should be pondered as to precisely what would have happened if this information had in fact been provided.

It is the completion of the instructions contained in Genesis 1:28, (including with regard to the enemy); that determines or will determine this date, and thus is subject to myriads of choices made by H. Sapiens. There is no possible way that the provision of this "date" as common knowledge, would have failed to change the behavior of individuals from that very time until today. (Today is pertinent, because "end times" has or have not yet happened.)

Thus these significant changes in behavior would have likely have altered this date, as compared to behavior of individuals *without* this information—thereby arguably proving God "wrong." Thus there is no way that God could provide this information, and at the same time have it remain accurate.

But of course God; being omniscient; would have likely factored these changes into His calculations prior to announcing the date. But would this have been fair to those who existed and lived their lives without this knowledge? It was bad enough that many of the "great men" of the Bible, seemingly unfairly passed on without salvation being available to them while they were alive. [See "*Ostium Ab Inferno—The Opening From Hell*"]

This begins to sound a bit like the predestination (religious determinism), vs. free will.

One cannot pour orange juice out of a container that contains only milk, as it contains no orange juice. If one wants to commit a crime and not get caught, it is best to commit a crime designed by someone else. The *details* of the design of the crime can only include that which is contained in the designer. Thus; the details of the crime provide much information about the nature of the *designer*, but not necessarily very much about the *perpetrator*.

A profile of the perpetrator would then necessarily include some attributes which the *designer* possesses, but the perpetrator does not possess. Likewise; in the *commission* of the crime, there would also be provided and thus include some attributes of the perpetrator, but not necessarily of the designer. If it is assumed by the authorities that the *perpetrator* of the crime also *designed* the crime; as opposed to the commission of a crime designed by someone else; no profile would ever fit particularly well. This helps to minimize the likelihood of getting caught.

God is free to act in any way He wishes, subject to His own rules. Man; being *created* in the image and likeness of God; is afforded the same freedom. It is the "rules" part that gets man into trouble— particularly the "equal and opposite reaction," or; "reaping what one sowed;" i.e.; the *karma* part.

> "God's will for the free will of man is
> both an absolute and non-absolute. It

is an absolute in the sense of man being completely free to make whatever choice(s) he wishes. And it is also an absolute, in that whatever is sown will ultimately be reaped. However; God's will for man's free will is also a non-absolute, in that interfering with another's free will provides the boundary. Thus free will, as is the case with many things, must be kept in balance."[3.10] [excerpt from *"Shâmar to Sharia"* Reprinted by Permission]

1 Corinthians 8:9 (KJV) tells us:

> *"But take heed lest by any means*
> *this liberty of yours*
> *become a stumbling block*
> *to them that are weak."*[3.11]

This sounds suspiciously like the first part of the previously cited James Madison quote: *"Liberty may be endangered by the abuse of liberty..."*—but of course Paul wrote it first.

This freedom or liberty was exemplified seemingly everywhere in the creation of the United States. It is throughout the founding documents, and appeared on the early coinage. In fact among early US coinage, is one example often referred to as the "liberty pole." The same depicts a "Phrygian cap," being carried on a pole. The Phrygian cap is reputed to be the symbol of a newly manumitted slave, here with the cap placed upon a pole to make certain no one "misses it." There exists a plethora of quotations regarding the fight for freedom. Clearly freedom was the main driving force for the formation of the country.

And; any and all "history revisionists" attempts notwithstanding; Freemasonry also played a vital role in the formation of this country. It must be remembered that in order to be a Freemason, one must be "freeborn;" meaning not a slave or indentured servant. In fact; some Masonic symbols still appear on US currency to this very day. The lodge notation for the recess at the time of the Boston Tea party was to: "break for tea" It must also be remembered that no legitimate Masonic lodge can open without a Holy Book.

Thus there exists an inextricable nexus between or among the formation of the United States, freedom, and God. After all, freedoms are rights endowed to man by his Creator.

But the statists see it a bit differently:

Once again: *"A statist government treats its political sovereignty as a platform for moral sovereignty. In other words, as ultimate sovereign, the state is therefore not subject to God the Bible natural law, or any other religion or ethical system."*

Three questions must be asked:
1) Precisely what is moral sovereignty?

2) Is there any difference between morality and a "cost benefit analysis;" and if so what is this difference?"

3) Precisely what is it that constitutes "upright" behavior?

These will now be addressed in reverse order:

Chapter 4

Morality, Ethics, and Statists

Although it is far beyond the scope of this work to address this in great detail; in response to the third question posed at the end of the previous chapter; *upright behavior* can be considered as: "that which is consistent with the vertical portion of man." Said vertical portion of man is that which "animates" him.

Genesis 2:7 (KJV) tells us:

> "*And the LORD God formed
> man of the dust of the ground,
> and breathed into his nostrils
> the breath of life;
> and man became a living soul.*"[4.1]

If the *material* portion of man, (here that which was *formed*), is considered to be the horizontal portion; then that which animates him or causes him to become a "*living soul*," (the breath of life), necessarily represents the vertical portion. During the time that these are united, (physical "life"); man is an upright or vertical being. When these are separated, (physical "death"); the material part of man then reverts to the horizontal. This union can be symbolized by the cross.

Upright behavior is that behavior which is consistent with that upright or vertical portion, which Genesis 2:7 tells us comes from God. This is as opposed to the "dust of the ground" portion. When man is "upright," this is the direct result of the inclusion of this "vertical" portion. Upright behavior can therefore reasonably be considered as that which is consistent with God.

What is it that is consistent with God? In the general sense, two primary "consistencies" with God are: *freedom* and *balance*.

As previously stated: "*The only criterion for limiting the expression of an individual's rights; is if said expression can reasonably be expected to interfere with the expression of another individual's rights.*"

Two seemingly identical actions can have entirely different results:

If someone visits a surgeon for the removal of a skin growth, and, with the patient's consent; the surgeon utilizes a knife to remove said growth; the balances are all *positive*. The patient is happy because the growth is gone; and the surgeon is likewise happy. [It must be noted that in a non-emergency situation, it is a *crime* in many jurisdictions to perform surgery without the consent of the patient.]

However; if in furtherance of a robbery, a perpetrator utilizes a similar knife; and makes the exact same incision on the victim, and serendipitously removes the exact same skin growth; all of the balances are now *negative*— except perhaps that the skin growth is gone. Here the perpetrator is subject to punishment by man, and has engaged in actions that will result in negative "equal and opposite reactions" or "karma." The victim is understandably traumatized, and may be able to file legal action in order to be compensated for the attack.

There are two main differences noted in these examples:

Firstly; is the *consent* of the patient vs. the *absence* of consent of the victim:

The patient sought out the surgeon for help. The exercise of the patient's free will was such that he consented to have the surgeon remove the growth surgically. The surgeon; respecting the free will of the patient; performed the procedure to the best of his or her ability, with the intention of *helping* the patient in a manner consistent with the will of the patient.

However, it must be remembered that the surgeon not only took into account the free will of the patient; but also what was in the patients best interests. Had the patient desired a procedure that the surgeon reasonably believed was not in the best interests of the patient, the surgeon would likely have refused.

This is *upright* behavior, and God does this all the time; and arguably He cannot do otherwise. Remember that high school sweetheart that was the "only one" for you? Remember how you felt when it didn't work out? You might have even been rather angry with God at the time. And remember when many years later you said: "Thank God." How *surgically* did God remove this person from your life? The answer is: as surgically as you would permit.

"But wait! God was not acting consistent with my will—I really wanted XYZ at that time." No; God respected your will, in that he stopped you from getting what you did not want. What you wanted was that which is; (actuality). What you had; was that which was not; as you only *thought*, (reality), that it was that *which is*. God respected your free will for what you actually desired; despite the fact that you were certain that you had it, but in actuality did not. He was able to understand your will and the fulfillment of the same, much better than you at that time. It was only years later when you realized this.

God will respect your free will and act accordingly; even if you are confused as to precisely what you think, (reality), it is that you want or have. And just like the surgeon, He will not help you attain that which is not in your best interest.

The victim of the aforementioned crime, did not wish to be robbed. Neither did this victim wish any type of surgery performed by the perpetrator in furtherance of the robbery. There was no consent stated or implied by the victim, for any changes to his or her current situation.

Secondly; is the *intentions* of the active parties:

The willful intentions of the surgeon; unlike the criminal; were to genuinely *help* the patient, at the expense of the surgeon's time and effort. The payment for the service merely compensates the surgeon for this; and generally is in no way any reflection of the value of the service to the patient. Here the patient receives benefit from the surgeon, which is of greater value to the patient than the fee. The surgeon benefits both financially, as well as in other areas.

The criminal on the other hand, desired to *harm* the victim. The criminal wanted to *gain* something at the *expense* of the victim; and to do so without the victim's consent—else he would simply have asked for the money. It was only through an unplanned, serendipitous, and unintentional concatenation of events that the growth was similarly removed. It was also for *harm*, or the threat of this harm, that the cutting instrument was utilized by the criminal.

The surgeon wanted to add value to the patient; and the criminal wanted to take away from the victim. To suggest that the criminal intending to *harm* the victim, but serendipitously *helping* the victim in the process of stealing money from the victim; is in *any* way analogous to actions of the surgeon, would be absurd.

The "*Second Intermission*" of "*MeekRaker Beginnings. . .*" provides a much more detailed and easily understandable explanation of this, but the "quickie" version is:

Actions by any being with self-awareness have two components:

The *first* is the material action; and the *second* is or are the reason(s) (exercise of free will) for this action.

Meaning that the *first* component, is *what* it is that is being done in the material; and the *second* component is *why* it is being done, or, what is or are the reason(s) for the action? It is the *product* of these two components, that determines both the true *magnitude* and the *polarity* of the action.

If the action is considered to be a force, it can be symbolized by the variable F. However as stated, F in actuality has two components: the *action*, and the *reason(s)* for the action. In order to illustrate and differentiate these, instead of F, the force is then better symbolized by the variable F_T with the subscript "T" meaning total; i.e.; total force.

The components of F_T are the *action* itself and the *reason*(s) for the action. The action can be symbolized by F_A, and the reason symbolized by F_R. Here the subscript "A" refers to the *action* part; with the subscript "R" referring to the *reason* for the action. As previously stated, the "actual action" is the product of these two components. This can be expressed as: $F_T = F_A \times F_R$.

If F_T is positive, then it is upright action. If F_T is negative, then it is not. These calculations assume that any given action itself or F_A, is always considered *positive* in polarity, because it exists. It further assumes that polarity of the *reason* can be determined; e.g.; *giving* is positive, and *stealing* is negative.

Just one more thing, as Newton proved "F = MA." Here "M" represents mass, and "A" represents acceleration. If F_T is substituted for F; we have $F_T = MA$. It is this "MA" that represents the "reap what you sow" law or karma, if combined with Newton's law of "equal and opposite reactions." The quantity and polarity of F_T results in an equal and opposite; (opposite here meaning *toward* the active party); reaction. The "M" represents the magnitude of the return, and the "A" represents how fast, (the acceleration of), the return manifests. There are an infinite number of combinations of "MA." How big the return is, and how fast it is returned is determined by God. A large return must take a long time, because "A" must be small if "M" is large in order to balance F_T. Likewise a fast return must be a smaller "M", because" "A" would then be large. What is important to know is that the *polarity* of "M" must be the same polarity of F_T.

The *second* question posed at the end of the previous chapter was: "*Is there any difference between morality and a "cost benefit analysis;" and if so what is this difference*?"

What is moral? Moral is: "directly from Latin *moralis* proper behavior of a person in society," literally "pertaining to manners."[4.2]

And precisely how is it that "proper behavior" is determined?

Before this can be determined, it is best to take a look at what constitutes a "cost benefit analysis (CBA)"?

This one seems pretty straightforward. If one goes to the supermarket to buy chicken, and one of the premium brands is on sale, but the other premium brand is not; which one is it that should be purchased? The one that is on sale of course— assuming that they are of equal quality. Why would one increase the *cost* by paying more for the same *benefit*?

This is strictly a logical and fact based conclusion. If two identical items are offered for sale, but one is substantially less expensive than the other; (less expensive is used here rather than cheaper; as *expense* refers to cost, while *cheap* refers to quality); why would one choose to pay more?

However when intangibles; e.g.; emotions; are factored in to the CBA analysis, things can get a bit confusing:

Q: "Why did you hit him?"
A: "Because he made me so D@%* mad."

Now there is a judge involved, and the "hitter" is wondering when the jail door will be unlocked; and has already been contacted by the attorney for the "hittee" about the medical bills, and much more.

So it must be asked if hitting the victim was worth what transpired afterward. Was the balancing of the anger by striking the victim "worth it?" Perhaps it was *emotionally* at the time, but certainly not presently. This was because this particular "cost benefit analysis," primarily factored emotion into the equation, as though it had some tangible value. However the jail cell is quite tangible, as are ultimately all of the other difficulties caused by this action.

Had the situation been different; meaning that it was a matter of self-defense, things would have been entirely different:

Q: "Why did you hit him?"
A: "Because I had no choice. He said that he was going to kill me, and began the process. It was either him or me."

This CBA was based upon reasonably perceived facts. Here it is not the "hitter," but rather the "hittee" who is in jail.

Things can also get confusing when there is lack of knowledge. Often times, there simply is not sufficient information available for a proper CBA, yet a decision must be made. So precisely how then is one able to make the best decision?

Moral is generally an adjective. Moral can also be a noun, if referring to something learned as the result of a story or anecdote. Morals (plural) can also refer to one's standards. *Morality* is a noun.

As previously stated, moral is: "directly from Latin *moralis* proper behavior of a person in society," literally "pertaining to manners." Thus it can be seen that "moral" et seq., refers to "proper behavior" or "pertaining to manners." The word "manner(s)" (if used in the plural) usually refers specifically to etiquette. But "manner" (in the singular) more generally refers to the *method* or a *means* by which something is done. Thus moral can refer to the *result*; or it can refer to the *means* by which a result is achieved; or both.

The exact quotation could not readily be found, so the following represents a paraphrased version of a quote from Robert A. Heinlein:

> *"When you do not know which choice represents the most moral, pick the most difficult choice, as that is usually the most moral."*

Why is it that one would want to choose the most moral course of action? The answer has already been stated. It is a matter of F = MA, and equal and opposite reactions. But that is only part of the answer.

The "proper behavior of a person in society," is that which ultimately causes the maximum good—if it is based upon truth. This maximum good disproportionally applies to the active party, because of the multiplicative capabilities of intent, or the *reason*, (F_R), for the action. It is this capability that can be responsible for the "hundredfold" return.

There are many rules and laws regarding both the material and immaterial realms, most of which as "rules and laws," remain yet unknown. The truth regarding "proper behavior," is contained in the Bible—most especially in the "*Book of Proverbs.*" It is because of the lack of *general* knowledge regarding "how things actually work—particularly in the *immaterial,*" that H. Sapiens are *advised* in the *specific* as to what constitutes moral behavior.

"If you give, you shall be given to;" and "If you take you shall be taken from;" represent specific instructions with respect to the aforementioned laws of F = MA, and equal and opposite reactions. These laws operate with many things, both in the material and in the immaterial realms. If these are known, they can then be applied to any decision. But since most do not know them; and of those that do, few understand or even believe that they apply in the *immaterial* realm; specific behavioral instructions or rules are necessary. Thus behavioral rules are to provide the maximum good—even if it does not seem that way at decision time.

When Jesus talked about treating others as one would wish to be treated, this was a behavioral rule based upon His knowledge of these laws. When He spoke of giving in order to receive, the same was true; despite the fact that many thought he was crazy at the time.

The "moral to the story," refers to understanding the rule or law taught by the "story." This includes the parables in the Bible. The problem is that man has "gotten his fingers" into them, often resulting in things that simply make no sense. A prime example being: the "Talent Man Story," as taught by Jesus. In the Monograph: "*Donald Trump*

Candidacy According to Matthew?" the truth of this parable is explained.

Suffice it to say, that the rules for behavior are based upon immutable laws of the material universe, and the immaterial realm whence they originated.

If something is truly moral, then it is necessarily upright.

The truly "inconvenient truth," is that the ends justify the means—*if and only if* the means justify the ends. And although emotions may be motivational, they are not a factor in these calculations.

The remaining question from the previous chapter is: "*What is moral sovereignty?*"

Again as previously stated:

> "*A statist government treats its political sovereignty as a platform for moral sovereignty. In other words, as ultimate sovereign, the state is therefore not subject to God the Bible natural law, or any other religion or ethical system.*"

First it must be asked precisely what is *sovereignty*—whether in the political, moral, or in any other sense?

The root of sovereignty is sovereign, and the etymology of sovereign is:

> "early 14c., "great, superior, supreme," from Old French *soverain* "highest,

supreme, chief," from Vulgar Latin
*superanus "chief, principal" (source
also of Spanish *soberano*, Italian
soprano), from Latin *super* "over" (see
super-). Spelling influenced by folk-
etymology association with *reign*"[4.3]

Thus with a *statist* view of government, "political
sovereignty" is a given. Statists believe that the
government is highest, or supreme reign. This
represents the antithesis of *governing* with the
consent of the governed, as the sovereign is never
the government, but those who actually posses the
power; and citizens can always: "Throw the bums
out."

Statists then attempt to extrapolate this
purported "political sovereignty" into "moral
sovereignty."

> *"If man were capable; either rindividually
> or collectively; of creating his own moral
> code; he would not need it. Men would
> then be angels."*[4.4]—*Emma B. Quadrakoff*

James Madison in Federalist Paper #51 tells us:

> *"If men were angels, no government
> would be necessary.
> If angels were to govern men,
> neither external nor internal controls
> on government would be necessary."*[4.5]

51

Madison is speaking here about controls on government. But the subsequent belief in governmental *moral* sovereignty, is the necessary outgrowth of an uncontrolled government. In fact it could reasonably be said that *by definition*; political sovereignty necessitates a government over which there cannot be any significant means of control.

Why is it that "men are not angels?" This question can be interpreted literally or non-literally. A literal answer could be "because they are not." But it is not so much the *structure* of angels that is the salient point. It is the *function* or *behavior* of angels, rather than their structure, that is germane. Even if the existence of angels is considered to be merely a "hypothetical construct;" much wisdom can nevertheless be gained from understanding what is believed to be true about them.

Angels; (hypothetical or actual); assist in the furtherance of the Creator's will. Angels assist in the furtherance of man's will, to the extent that the same does not conflict with the will of the Creator. This is actually the same rule that applies to man, and angelic purpose likely predates this. However; angels are bound to *not* act in a manner that interferes with the will of the Creator. Man is not *supposed* to act in a manner that interferes with the will of another man, as this also interferes with the Creator's will for man's free will. Does this mean that man cannot act against the will of another man and/or the Creator? Of course not;

but only that no *angelic* assistance should be expected in acting against the will of either.

Government is the exception to this rule. By giving *consent* to be governed, man agrees to some degree of interference with his expression of free will, in furtherance of a greater good. Without the consent of the governed, *individual* free will remains superior to any purported *collective* free will—any purported belief to the contrary notwithstanding.

Except perhaps once, when the "one third" may have left, (which is actually not true); angels are not subject to the influence of the enemy. However many did in fact leave, these are no longer angels; and have had substantial diminution of their angelic powers—particularly at Calvary. [An alternate but nevertheless fair read of the story of "Legion," is that some *demons* were in fact "saved," and returned to "angelic duty;" with the same being the reason for the inclusion of the story.[4.6] see "*MeekRaker Beginnings. . .*"]

Thus (true) angels act in furtherance of the Creator's will, and also in furtherance of the will of man; to the extent that the same is also consistent with the Creator's will, and is balanced. Angels; if they are to remain angels; can thus refuse to "help" man; but are not, (if they are angels), subject to the influence of the enemy—*they cannot sin.*

As previously stated, God's will is for the free will of man, to the extent that one man's will does not interfere with another's. God's desire for free will of man, is such that his even includes the "right" to sin; and obtain the balance for said sin.

This alone would provide substantial basis for the enemy to take the opposite approach; meaning—because God wants free will for man, the enemy does not. However it is much more than that. The enemy actually believes he can defeat and supplant God.

The *Divine* method of helping H. Sapiens to make upright decisions, is *education* in both the particulars of the situation; and the knowledge of consequences as outlined above, (equal and opposite reactions). Actualities can never be fully perceived by man; so for man, the *reality* of any actuality is always less than complete. This is why there is a "moral code;" in order to provide guidance when information is insufficient.

But the enemy believes in no such thing. He practices *manipulation*, via lies and emotional pressure. His goal is to manipulate H. Sapiens into doing *his* will. And he is fully cognizant of "equal and opposite reactions," often using this to his benefit.

This is seen in Job 1:10-12 (KJV):

"Hast not thou made an hedge about him, and about his house, and about all that he hath on every side?

thou hast blessed the work of his hands, and his substance is increased in the land.

54

*But put forth thine hand now,
and touch all that he hath,
and he will curse thee to thy face.*

*And the LORD said unto Satan,
Behold, all that he hath is in thy
power; only upon himself put
not forth thine hand.
So Satan went forth from the
presence of the LORD."*[4-7]

Here Satan is seeking permission from God to
attack Job. Satan is complaining about the "hedge"
that God has made around Job, and Satan wants it
lowered. Satan is also complaining about Job being
"blessed" and Job's "substance is increased." The
same was because of, and the direct result of, the
positive "equal and opposite" reactions to Job's
faith and actions.

The reason that God partially consents to Satan's
desires, is because Job had to some extent also
been practicing *fear* instead of faith. Job had been
making "offerings" as an "insurance policy" because
of the *suspected* behavior of his offspring. It
cannot be overlooked that Job himself was still
inside this "hedge;" with the same being lowered
for "all that he hath;" but not for his *person*, as no
"hand" of Satan was to be put upon Job "himself."

The interplay of forces can be seen here, with the
blessings being given to Job, because he was a man
of faith and acted "uprightly." "Given" does not
accurately describe these blessings, as they were

earned. The negative actions of Job with respect to his fears, provided, or better stated, *earned* negative imbalances; which were balanced by God's qualified and limited permission to Satan.

H. Sapiens are the greatest known "creation" in the universe. The chain of authority is God, then H. Sapiens, and then angels; and in that precise order. This is actuality.

But the enemy does not see it that way. Or perhaps better stated; he *knows* this, but does not like it. Instead; he engages in delusional behavior, believing that it is he who is or will be God, and H. Sapiens; who he knows full well rank higher than he; are in fact merely "useful idiots." Satan's job is to abolish free will, lest said "idiots" discover the truth. Instead; since the free will and the truth will not help him; he is involved with *manipulation* of H. Sapiens in furtherance of his delusional desires.

Henry Kissinger once described the Soviet Union, as a thief walking down a hotel hallway; checking doorknobs in order to try and find those which were not locked; in order to steal from these unlocked rooms. The enemy does precisely the same; and there are reasons for this similarity.

Either only one man or no man ever escaped manipulation by the enemy—depending on whether or not one believes in Jesus. The truth is that this attempt at manipulation by the enemy; i.e.; "rattling the doorknobs;" is 24/7. And there are always some unlocked doors.

Once again: "*A statist government treats its political sovereignty as a platform for moral sovereignty. In other words, as ultimate sovereign, the state is therefore not subject to God the Bible natural law, or any other religion or ethical system."*

By design and in this usage, it is inarguable that the structure of the US government, is such that it is deliberately structured to make the true sovereign the people.

Therefore any claim that the US government as currently structured, can ever be the true sovereign, is without merit.

Therefore any purported "platform" proffered as a prerequisite for "moral sovereignty," simply does not exist.

Ergo; no such "moral sovereignty" exists; or can exist in this, or any other "upright" system of government.

"Quis Custodiet Ipsos Custodes?" Sometimes translated as: "Who watches the watchers?" or "Who will guard the guards themselves?" The answer of course must be the people.

And what about: the logic of: *"as ultimate sovereign, the state is therefore not subject to God the Bible natural law, or any other religion or ethical system."*

This represents a kind of "if then" statement. Here stated with the presumption that the "as" or "because," (the "if" condition) has already been met contextually; (the state as the ultimate sovereign); thus what follows (after the "therefore") is thus purported as truth.

However; given the impossibility of any person or persons to be the "ultimate sovereign;" whatever is concluded is "therefore" not only not true, but *necessarily* false.

The presumption of a God or a "Creator" as the "ultimate sovereign," forms the basis for the "social contract" known as the US government; and this contract was accepted with this understanding.

Thus it matters little if one believes there is no God, with respect to the provisions of said "contract." One cannot usurp this "ultimate sovereign," simply because one does not believe that the previously agreed upon "ultimate sovereign" exists. No individual or group of individuals has the authority to abrogate this "contract," except as provided for in the same.

In a sense; God, the Bible; (if and when read correctly); and natural law are "severally and jointly" one in the same.

Before the "In the Beginning;" there *was*, but there also *was not*. Science partially recognizes and understands this. Science admits that before the beginning, there was not yet that which now is; i.e.; the material realm.

That which "now is," began "In the Beginning." This necessitates that there *was* such an entity as the *immaterial* realm, often translated as "heaven;" but never *correctly* translated as "the heavens." Immaterial is correct here, as it is the *material* realm that was *not* prior to the "Beginning," but now is.

Before "The Beginning," there was God, and the immaterial realm in which He resides; which again can be referred to as "heaven," but not "the heavens." After "The Beginning," there was and still is "God and the immaterial realm in which He resides;" which can be referred to as "heaven." But now, (or then; i.e.; after The Beginning); there is or was also the *material* universe including the celestial bodies; along with "the heavens;" essentially referring to the space between the celestial bodies. This was also the beginning of time. One cannot have motion, without time, (and space) references. One cannot have any "Beginning," without a time reference.

Thus there is only one "place," and one entity, whence material or *natural* law *could* originate. "Natural law," is that which is often observed, (and more often not observed); regarding that which was created. [Supernatural law refers to the laws in or of the immaterial realm from which the material realm was created. Natural laws are derived from and are a subset of supernatural law. However there are immaterial laws that do not apply in the material such as regarding the lack of time and space, neither of which existed until created "In the Beginning."]

Thus these "natural laws" represent the "rules" regarding that which was created. Therefore it follows that the *source* of both that which *was* created, (including its laws); and that *which* created, is the same.

To the extent that it is translated and understood correctly; the Bible represents among many other things, a subset of: "what He did and said." Although the primary purpose of the Bible is neither physics nor history, but rather *redemption*; it nevertheless contains some small degree of history, and some explanations of some "natural," and also some explanations of some "supernatural" laws. Unless this distinction is well understood, things can easily become quite confusing.

The title of "ultimate sovereign" can only be properly applied to *that which created*; and can *never* be ascribed to *that which was created*; in any absolute, ultimate, or even meaningful sense—as no creation can ever be greater than its creator.

And that which *created*, necessarily and simultaneously created the *rules* regarding that which was created. In fact it can be stated that said rules or laws are necessary for maintaining that which was created; and actually it is unclear as to which actually came first. An electrical circuit—even one as simple as two wires attached to a light bulb; create the "rules" for the flow of that energy we know as electricity. If these "rules" are changed, then the result will necessarily change.

The Creator cannot *arbitrarily* change the rules for that which was created, and yet maintain the same creation. "God can do anything" is better stated as: "God can do anything that can be done." He cannot arbitrarily cause the sum of 2 plus 2 to equal 100 when one deposits funds into their bank account; but then cause the sum to equal 1 when these same funds are withdrawn. This is not to say that He cannot achieve the same *effect*, but only that it cannot be arbitrary; i.e.; it must somehow be balanced or "paid for"—else atoms as we know them would also simultaneously cease to exist. Believing otherwise often results in grave disappointments about God.

Yet somehow statists, if and when in power, and at most having only arguably oxymoronic and temporary "relative sovereignty;" nevertheless believe that they are not subject to these same rules. This is clearly evidenced by their behavior.

This is seen with the burdensome regulatory schemes applied to US businesses, who are nevertheless somehow supposed to successfully compete with foreign businesses not subject to the same. Or with the expenditures of the same monies twice—the same monies being spent both for Medicare *and* "private" health insurance subsidies at the same time. This brings to mind the simple question asked her brother by Dagny Taggart in "*Atlas Shrugged*:" "How Jim?"

The way that a statist approaches that which exists, seems to be from a hierarchical viewpoint. From a quasi Orwellian viewpoint: "All men are created equal, but some are created more equal;" would be the mantra of the statist—thereby assuming that one of the two is superior to the other. Of course this is nonsense, as when two things that are equal, one cannot by definition be superior to the other, with respect to that quality or quantity for which there is equality.

Thus irrespective of any purported beliefs to the contrary, statists believe in a hierarchy of H. Sapiens. The statist considers himself as superior to "normal men." Therefore it is the statist's obligation and duty to act as a "shepherd" for the "flocks," who "need" and "welcome" such guidance.

Thus in the mind of the statist, the purpose of political leadership positions is to do whatever the statist believes is best for these flocks; rather than to be a representative of the people, and acting in accordance with, and in furtherance of, the will of these same people.

Thus statism is not truly political, but rather is an issue of *control* via politics, and is based upon a much more primary belief. Just as political progressivism is not political, but rather a tactic or a strategy depending upon the situation; statism also is not so much political, but rather a matter of self-proclaimed *positioning*; merely utilizing the political as a *means* to their ends.

Given their believed superiority over "mere mortals," statists either deliberately and/or with ignorance, often cite Biblical principles in furtherance of their ends. This represents classic sophistry.

The instructions contained in the Bible regarding such things as feeding the hungry, clothing the naked, caring for the poor, etc.; are provided to *individuals* both for the benefit of those in need; and also ultimately for and to the benefit of the "giver."

Because of the *reason* for the giving (F_R), the individual giver will reap rewards for the act of giving according to $F = MA$, and equal and opposite reactions. Because the giver wishes to help another, this product, (F_R x F_A), will be returned to the giver to the giver's benefit. This is precisely why God loves a "cheerful giver." This represents the exercise of free will, in order to help those in need.

This same system is also maintained with legitimate forms of "collective giving;" i.e.; legitimate charities and churches. Here various types of groups are formed in order to facilitate "giving." Individuals willingly *choose* to transfer some portion of their wealth to these groups, who then distribute this wealth to those in need. These groups are formed to provide "economies of scale," so that there is a more efficient means of giving. Most importantly, this represents the exercise of man's *free will*, in order to help those in need.

However when the government gets involved, everything changes. Wealth is expropriated from individuals, and then said wealth is spent according to the desires of those in political power.

Ergo; the "giver" is not really a giver at all. The giver "gives" because he is *required* to as a matter of law; and this is being done mainly to avoid serious penalties. This is *not* an act of free will, and is not being done to help those in need; but rather to avoid harm to the giver. The giver has little say in where these expropriated monies are spent, other than by voting—too often being forced to choose between two, and only two, almost equally unacceptable alternatives.

This must be distinguished from taxation in order to fund governmental operations. Obviously, some forms of taxation are required in order to fund the activities of any legitimate or "just" government. These monies are *properly* or *justly* utilized, only when they are used to *fund* legitimate expenditures; and not for the *transfer* of wealth from individual to individual.

As can easily be seen, the "equal and opposite reactions" created as the result of sending wealth under duress to a governmental entity; are entirely different from those obtained from willfully, (and cheerfully), donating to a cause of one's own choosing. Here the return is much less for the giver; and practically nonexistent or even negative for the politicians who are giving away other peoples wealth—wealth that was obtained by the government via *duress*, or "under penalty of law."

And for whatever it is worth, those portions of taxes that are used by the *government* to redistribute wealth; unlike charitable contributions, are not tax deductible.

This leads to an interesting point: When individual contributions to help others *are deducted*, this changes the dynamics substantially. Why? Because any monies that the giver receives back because of deducting a charitable contribution, is ultimately paid by others. Any monies received by the giver from the tax deduction of any charitable contribution that he would otherwise not have received as a taxpayer; are being paid (subsidized) unknowingly and without the consent of other taxpayers—even if first borrowed. This not only reduces the *effective* amount of the contribution, (F_A), with respect to the "equal and opposite reaction; but also sets up an additional but *negative* return because of this forced subsidy. Deducting charitable contributions thus represents a perceived gain in the short term, but in actuality represents a diminution of the long term benefit to the giver.

Thus any statist who believes that either he or the government of which he approves, or any other person or government, is: *"not subject to God the Bible natural law,"* is at best delusional.

The "fatal flaw" of this position can easily be demonstrated in the natural. If this were so; then if any statist accidentally hits his thumb with a hammer, there would be no need for the utterance of any expletives. To even suggest that this were true, reminds one of the episodes of the *"Adventures of Superman."* There Jimmy is wearing "the magic necklace," which he believes protects him from any and all harm—At least until Lois kicks him in the shins and Jimmy exclaims: "That hurt!" and then promptly faints.

With respect to the statist's purported immunity to *"any other religion or ethical system;"* the first purported immunity; (to religion); in certain senses is arguably true. In fact, no political leaders should ever engage in any official promulgation of any religion. Of all of the possible evil forms of government, a theocracy is likely the worst, [See Monograph: *"Shâmar to Sharia"*]; and the founding fathers knew this very well.

With respect to any purported immunity to "ethical system(s);" this however is another matter.

What is or are ethics?

Despite general conflation, and the assumption that "ethics" is synonymous with "morals;" this is untrue. Although ethics are related to morality, in that long term consequences are the primary consideration, they are quite different. Morality has previously been addressed. So then what is or are ethics?

Ethics is much more concerned with the *circumstances* surrounding the act, rather than the very act itself. Meaning that an act can fit into four combinations with respect to ethics and morals: An act can be moral and ethical; immoral and yet ethical; moral and unethical or immoral and unethical.

For example: A physician hugging a grieving patient; would generally be considered as both a moral and an ethical act.

For this same physician, to tell an obscene joke to a patient, could be considered as immoral; but yet perfectly ethical, depending upon intent.

For this same physician, to; even in a gentlemanly and highly respectful manner; (split infinitive(s) noted); ask a patient for a "date;" might be a highly moral, but yet an extremely unethical act.

And for this same physician, (for sure if married); to engage in "extra-curricular physical activities;" (euphemism noted); with a patient, would be both immoral and highly unethical.

Unlike as is the case with ethics; "morality" can at times vary somewhat depending upon cultures, and the needs of the same. A culture that for whatever reasons(s), were to lose say 90% of its male population, might have to alter that which is considered "moral"—if the survival of the culture is the prime issue. Long term results can affect what is considered "moral." This is despite the misunderstanding regarding morality being simply an "obstacle to fun."

And in the aforementioned circumstances, what was once considered as a "desirable" activity; might *now* become considered a burden. Here what is now considered to be the moral thing; might very well be the antithesis of that which was once considered as moral.

But "ethics" has or have no such latitude. "Ethical" is much more of a binary. Prior to attaining the "age of majority;" i.e.; an adult; many activities are either prohibited, or have no legal status; e.g.; the signing of a contract.

A "minor" is not permitted by law to engage in certain activities. Sometimes it is the *minor* that is subject to serious legal penalties for engaging in, or even attempting to engage in certain activities.

Sometimes the minor is allowed to engage in certain activities with another minor; but not engage in the same or similar activities with one who *is* of the age of the majority. Here in this case, it is the *adult* who is generally subject to serious punishment.

This is based both upon "free will" and "informed consent." It is understood that although minors have the capability to make decisions in certain areas, they nevertheless lack the capabilities to understand the ramifications of decisions made in other areas. Thus; they are prohibited from the same.

Although this is sound rationale, the system is imperfect. As of this writing; it is currently the law in most areas, that although a person has "enough on board" to understand the ramifications of carrying a machine gun, killing human beings, and potentially losing his or her life on behalf of his country; he or she yet nevertheless somehow lacks sufficient judgment to enjoy a glass of beer with his or her pizza. The level of wisdom, understanding, and judgment required to drink that beer, is generally not to be considered as attainable for another three years.

Free will is meaningless, if is there is inadequate understanding of the nature of the decision and the ramifications of the same. Ethics is concerned with the *reality* or *perception* of the facts, and or circumstances surrounding a judgment or decision. Something is unethical, when any other party to the decision reasonably has any type advantage; or even the *appearance* of any type of advantage over the person making the decision.

Although a bit different, this is similar to the situation regarding minors. With respect to minors, it is the inability to ascertain the ramifications of a decision, because of lack of "maturity."

With respect to ethics, it is misinformation, or a misperception (faulty reality), of actuality by the party; (victim); that is likely to cause them to make an erroneous decision, (see psychological transference). This existence of misperception, (and likely subsequent erroneous decision), must be *presumed* by the active person or persons who have, or even may simply *appear* too have any type of advantage.

A doctor cannot date a patient, because the patient's perception of the doctor is different than it would be if the *circumstances* were different. Meaning; because of the doctor/patient relationship, the patient is and must be *presumed* to be incapable of accurate perceptions, and thus any accurate free will decision in certain matters.

If it had been the case that this same patient had met the same "doctor" under different circumstances, ethics might not be an issue. Meaning; had the "patient" simply met the "doctor" at a grocery store, with no knowledge of this person's profession and was not "their doctor;" there would be no ethical concerns if the "doctor" asked him or her for a "date."

If it were the case that the "doctor" was married, there would be *moral* concerns; but not ethical concerns. It must be noted however, that for the very same aforementioned reasons; the person would be less likely to agree to the date; as the "position" of "doctor;" i.e.; "their doctor," would not be utilized in their decision making process.

Attorneys have even more strict ethical concerns. In addition to any misperceptions of actuality because of the attorney/client relationship as with a physician, there is also the matter of knowledge. Meaning; that attorneys generally cannot represent a person in a matter against another person whom they have previously represented. One reason for this; is because said attorney may have information he or she would not otherwise have, as the result of a previous attorney/client relationship with that person they had previously worked "for," but now would be working "against."

Years ago, a US president who was involved in a "mess" with an intern stated:

> *"I think I did something for the worst*
> *possible reason; just because I could. I*
> *think that's the most, just about the*
> *most morally indefensible reason that*
> *anybody could have for doing*
> *anything."*[4.8]—Bill Clinton

Once again "morally" and "ethically" are easily conflated. The actions in question here concern both. What was done was highly unethical, because of the circumstances. One party was the President, and the other a young female intern. Was the intern capable of a competent free will decision regarding the actions? Or: was it the case that the intern was "star-struck" because of the position of the other party? How much of her decision was based upon the fact that the other party was the president? If she had met the same person in the aforementioned grocery store, and had no idea of his position; would the outcome have been the same?

Although some might argue that this intern knew quite well what she was doing, and was actually interested in fame; this does nothing to change the ethical responsibilities of the person "in power." Unlike is or was the case with *morality*, it was not the responsibility of the intern to recognize how *unethical* this was. The intern is *presumed*, or *should be presumed*, to have no such knowledge or responsibility.

And of course what was done was highly immoral for both parties. He was married and she was quite aware of this fact. Even if the most liberal construction of "morality" with regard to these types of actions is stipulated; there nevertheless remains the fact that he was married.

However; although the use of: "the most morally indefensible reason" may seem erroneous; and that this should have been more correctly referred to as "the most ethically indefensible reason;" this is not necessarily the case in this usage. Ethical lapses such as these are in fact also "morally indefensible;" because of the long term results.

Whenever the *capability*, ("because I could"), is the basis for choosing an action; this itself is often antithetical to morality. As previously stated, generally the most difficult choice is usually the most moral. This is because one has to forfeit any perceived short term gains, for long term consequences. With respect to this particular matter; given all that transpired as a direct result of what happened, and if he had known this at the time; and if he could "do it all over again," would his actions be the same?

Back to the statists: It is not surprising, that statists claim immunity to any ethical requirements, as they must. The very bases of their beliefs are antithetical to the very concept of ethics.

Statists genuinely believe that they are the superior beings, whose destiny it is to coerce all less worthy beings into "proper" actions. "Proper" here meaning that which statists believe at any given time is "proper." Statists believe that it is not their role to govern, but rather to *rule*.

At the time of the initial *creation* of man from *nothing*, (Hebrew: bârâ); as well as at the time of the *formation*, (Hebrew: yâtsar), of Adam from *something*, (Hebrew: 'âphâr); there seems to be no evidence of God compelling any man to be subservient to any other man or men. The original *created* hosts were instructed/commanded to put the kibosh, (Hebrew: kâbash), on the earth, but it seems no "hierarchies" were ever established at that time.

Later the Commandments were established, but at least where they first appear in the Scriptures, (Exodus 20); God never even required obedience, but rather (only) to *shâmar* the same. This means to "keep" them, not as in *obey*; but to *protect* them as though surrounded by a "hedge of thorns;" thus being readily available for reference and utilization in decision making processes. Thus the Commandments were provided as a means of *education* consistent with free will, rather than any type of *coercion*.

Given man's free will to sin, it is obvious that any actual *compulsion* by God is in fact impossible under God's system, as this is antithetical to true free will. Man has the free will to do anything that he is capable of doing, whether sinful or upright— with the understanding that whatever is sown will be reaped. Obviously this is God's will; else He would simply make or would have made behavior inconsistent with His will impossible.

Free will, is God's guiding principle, along with the understanding of balance; i.e.; equal and opposite reactions. Any purported subrogation of free will by man, must be done as a *free will* decision; i.e.; with the *consent* of the governed; in order to be consistent with God's will.

What is *inconsistent* with God's will; is the *coercion* of any type of behavior by man, without willful prior (informed) consent of man in some form or another.

However; God is not the only entity in the universe capable of influencing man's behavior. This leads to observations which many might find a bit uncomfortable—

Chapter 5

Interference

Scriptures and science both agree that: "In the beginning, the heavens and the earth were created." The disagreement begins with the *causative* factor.

The Scriptures tell us that it was *God* who created the heavens and the earth. Science proffers no knowledge with regard to the active party, (the *primum movens* or prime mover), in this creation.

Once again; the terms *creation* and *creator* means to bring forth something from *nothing*, (no material thing); as was the case in the creation of the heavens and earth, and the original created hosts. Again; this is in contradistinction to making something out of something else; (existing matter). This; (making something out of something else); was largely the case with what transpired with respect to the earth after the word "earth" appears at the end of Genesis 1:1. This is also what happened with respect to the *formation* of both Adam and Eve, and remains the method of human reproduction today.

Genesis 1:1 clearly states that the earth was created "In the Beginning;" and the last word of Genesis 1:1 is in fact "earth." This "In the Beginning" is considered by most to be considered "real time" for what follows. Meaning; it is (erroneously) believed, that Genesis 1:2 onward for quite some "time," refers to this "Beginning" contemporaneously, with much of the same representing merely a more detailed recapitulation of Genesis 1:1; i.e.; "intra-beginning" events.

The alternative explanation being, that it was the creation of the "heavens and the earth," and the creation of the "heavens and the earth" *only* that occurred "In the Beginning."

Here this "Beginning," strictly refers to the creation of the heavens and the earth, and the "Beginning" of time, space, and matter. Once the heavens and earth were "created," this "Beginning" was concluded.

Thus here the reader is placing himself or herself *not* (real time), at or *during* the "Beginning:" but rather at the time the events *from Genesis 1:2 onward* occurring as present or "real time" when *read*; with the events that occurred "In the Beginning," having happened a long time ago in the *past*. Here any and all events after Genesis 1:1, are considered as "extra-beginning" events

With this approach, the earth was completed at an unspecified time, long before its condition as described in Genesis 1:2. Thus the condition of the earth as described in Genesis 1:2, represents a *change* from its *original*, (perfect), status; as described at the end of Genesis 1:1. It must be remembered that the Interlinear Bible translates Genesis 1:2 as: "she *became* without form and void."[5.1] (emphasis added) [It is beyond the scope of this work to litigate this position, but the exhaustive and irrefutable arguments for this position can be found in "*MeekRaker Beginnings. . .*"]

This *effect* of a change in status of the earth required a *cause*. If God did it; then for some reason He must have somehow and for some reason(s), changed His mind with respect to what the earth should be. If God did not change his mind; then something or someone else must have done it; i.e.; something else other than God caused these changes as described in Genesis 1:2.

Revelation 12:7-9 (KJV) tells us:

"And there was war in heaven:
Michael and his angels fought
against the dragon;
and the dragon fought and his angels,
And prevailed not; neither
was their place
found any more in heaven.

And the great dragon was cast out,
that old serpent, called the Devil,
and Satan, which deceiveth

the whole world:
he was cast out into the earth,
and his angels were cast
out with him."[5.2]

The book of Revelation is actually called "The Apocalypse." Despite the fact that the "Apocalypse" is often believed to be synonymous with "end times," or "Armageddon;" (which actually refers to a "final" battle *location*); this is an erroneous usage.

There are two related words: Apocrypha and Apocalypse. The first; *apocrypha*; although today generally referring to non-authenticated books of the Bible; actually is better translated as "hidden things;" as in something that is "cryptic." The second word, *apocalypse*, (apocalypsa); generally means "revealed things." Hence the translation of what was originally "The Apocalypse," is now known as: "The Book of Revelation."

John wrote the Apocalypse as the result of being permitted to "see" in the immaterial realm; i.e.; "heaven," (but not "the heavens"). This immaterial realm currently exists, and existed prior to the "Beginning" referenced in Genesis 1:1. It was from this realm that God created the heavens and the earth. It had to be, since the two realms; immaterial and material; are a binary in that there is either matter or there is not—and simple logic tell us that nothing can reside in a realm not yet created.

In this *immaterial* realm, there is neither time nor distance; with these manifesting only with God's creation of the material realm. Matter is in motion, and motion requires time and distance.

Thus what it was that John witnessed simultaneously, was that which already happened; that which was happening; and that which was yet to happen. Revealing these is known as: *retrophesy*, (author's terminology), if revealing unknown events from the *past*; *news* or current events, if revealing unknown events *currently*. (real time), happening; and *prophesy*, if revealing unknown events about that which *will* happen in the *future*. *Prescience* is the *possessing* of knowledge beforehand; and *prophesy* is *stating* this knowledge beforehand. Unless this is clearly understood; understanding "*The Book of Revelation*," necessarily becomes monumentally more difficult than it is when this *is* understood.

Adding to the "time warp" confusion, is the lack of terminology available to John in describing phenomena that almost no one else has ever "seen." Most cultures do not have words to describe things that do not exist, and/or no one even believes exist. This is why John was forced to use terms such as "like" or "as;" often misinterpreted as similes; but in actuality were attempts at *literal* descriptions; using the closest, (most synonymic), terminology available to him. In addition; there are also the *errors in translation* regarding specifically what it was that these phenomena resembled to John.

Thus although "Revelation," is generally considered to consist of prophesy only, this is not so. This is why some of the events contained in or described in Revelation, are so similar to other events recorded in the Bible—irrespective of whether or not John had previous knowledge of these *past* events at the time. Revealed things or *apocalypse*, refers to knowledge revealed, and is not limited to future events only. Moses is believed to have written Genesis, describing events long before his birth, (retrophesy).

The specific events described above in Revelation 12:7-9, are likely not events which will happen in the future (*prophesy*); but rather are likely a description of what has already happened (*retrophesy*); at some point between Genesis 1:1 and Genesis 1:2.

Isaiah 14:12 (KJV) tells us:

> *"How art thou fallen from heaven,*
> *O Lucifer, son of the morning!*
> *how art thou cut down to the ground,*
> *which didst weaken the nations!"*[5.3]

Here it seems that Isaiah is describing the very events described in Revelation 12:7-9. It must be noted that the same is presented here in Isaiah in the *past* tense. However; one might argue that since Isaiah was a *prophet*; i.e.; one with *prescience*; there may have merely been a translational error with respect to the tense.

Of course one could also argue that if this happened long before Isaiah was born, this would then in fact represent *retrophesy*, rather than prophesy.

The exclamation point at the end of the first sentence is worthy of mention. Since the books of Bible are believed to have been written in continuous form with no punctuation, this likely was added. Some may believe that it should have been a question mark. Even if so, this would nevertheless still represent an inquiry about a past event.

Luke 10:18-20 (KJV) tells us:

> *"And he said unto them,*
> *I beheld Satan as lightning*
> *fall from heaven.*
> *Behold, I give unto you power to tread*
> *on serpents and scorpions,*
> *and over all the power of the enemy:*
> *and nothing shall by any*
> *means hurt you.*
>
> *Notwithstanding in this rejoice not,*
> *that the spirits are subject unto you;*
> *but rather rejoice,*
> *because your names*
> *are written in heaven."*[5.4]

Here Jesus is first describing events that are also in the past. He is also describing the "chain of command," with regard to the "helpers" of the enemy, as well as *"power... over all the power of the enemy."* The inclusion of *"all"* should be noted.

But clearly Jesus states that he knew of at least parts of the events which appear to be described in Revelation 12:7-9. It cannot be overlooked that He; just as did Isaiah; stated "heaven," as in the *immaterial* realm; and not "the heavens," which is essentially the space between the celestial matter in the *material* realm. Thus without any doubt; at the time Jesus made these statements, the enemy had long since been cast down to the earth—any and all arguments that Revelation is solely concerned with future events notwithstanding.

This is why in Genesis 1:28 God told the created hosts to: *"replenish the earth, and subdue it: and have dominion over the fish of the sea, and over the fowl of the air, and over every living thing that moveth upon the earth."* By the time of Genesis 1:2, the completed "earth" referenced at the end of Genesis 1:1, had undergone substantial changes as the result of the enemy not so much being "cast out," but rather where he "ended up."

This represents the introduction of the player who is responsible for "all that is *not* of God," at lease in two possible ways:

Firstly; we are told in the above Revelation 12:7-9: *"And the great dragon was cast out, that old serpent, called the Devil, and Satan, which deceiveth the whole world."* This is presented not as what *will* or *would* happen; but what was happening or happened *at that time*—at the time John "witnessed" it.

82

In Isaiah 14:12 it is the word "*fallen*," (past tense); and *not* "falling," or "will fall," that appears.

And in Luke 10:18-20, the word "*beheld*," (past tense) appears.

Decisions must be made regarding the use of tenses in the translations.

Was this stated from *John's* perspective at the time? Meaning: that John knew quite well of the "current" machinations of the enemy. Thus in writing of these in the *present* tense, (deceiveth); was this written from the perspective of what had happened and what continues to happen, in John's experience; i.e.; that there was deception *now*, but no actual deception prior to the casting out? If so; what then were the actions that resulted in the "casting out?"

As an aside, there is also an interesting, but seemingly unintentional explanation of another phenomenon contained in these passages. The same being that there is no place in heaven for that which is not of God. In these passages, Satan was originally in the immaterial; hence when he or it exhibited behavior that was not of God, he or it had to be "cast out." H. Sapiens are in a bit of a different situation. Since the combination of material and immaterial known as H. Sapiens are *not* residents solely of the immaterial realm; there is no need to cast them out if behavior that is not of God is exhibited. Instead; H. Sapiens are simply not permitted re-entry. God cannot be contaminated by that which is not of God—hence man's need for salvation by justification. It is at least arguable that as previously stated, this is the reason the story (not a parable) concerning Legion is included in the New Testament.

Or is this written in an absolute sense? Meaning; that there were in fact "material realm" deceptions occurring prior to the "casting out." If so, then it must be asked precisely *who* it was on earth that Satan was deceiving prior to Genesis 1:2—the rocks? We are in fact told in the previous Revelation 12:7-9: *"which deceiveth the whole world: he was cast out into the earth, and his angels were cast out with him."*

Clearly we are told that there is a relationship between the deception and the casting out; irrespective of whether or not said relationship is *causal*, (not casual); or merely an issue of *timing*. Meaning: that although it is not clearly stated that said deception was the *cause* for the casting out, it is clear that deception had occurred *prior* to the casting out.

In addition; if so, said deceptions must have then necessarily been happening from heaven or the *immaterial* realm, here in this passage referred to as *"heaven;"* (but not "the heavens"). Satan then was and had been, (material reference), deceiving the *"whole world"* from the immaterial realm prior to being "cast out."

Precisely what is that which is described as the "whole world?" No evidence can be found which even remotely suggests that there is any other meaning other than the entire world. Satan was deceiving the entire material earth; and necessarily all of that which was on the earth; while he was still in the immaterial realm.

Then there is that which at first may seem silly, until it becomes evident that it is also more than arguably irreconcilable: There is time where time exists; and there is no time where time does not exist. The same can be said of space, distance, and matter. Thus reconciling the "chain of events" in the material, with "corresponding," or "cause and effect" events in the realm where there is no time, space, distance, or matter; seems impossible to the human mind.

Secondly; there is a change noted in the second part. Satan was "*cast out into the earth.*" From this point onward, Satan was no longer operating from the immaterial realm; but rather from the material (earth) realm. [The "*into*" part is beyond the scope of this work.]

Although this is also beyond the scope of this work, the latter; (*absolute* sense; i.e.; there were in fact "material realm" deceptions occurring prior to the "casting out"); strongly suggests some type of "life form(s)" be present on the earth between Genesis 1:1 and Genesis 1:2—else what was the target of the deception? What God actually and literally did during that which is known as the "creation;" (as opposed to, and *after* conclusion of the "Beginning"); is consistent with this possibility.

Most believe that early Genesis is fraught with "creating." However an unbiased analysis of the actual events based upon actual terminology, strongly suggests otherwise.

"Words mean things, and perfect synonyms are difficult, especially in translations. Actually, it is not certain that there are any perfect synonyms within the same language. "In the Beginning," it was the heavens and the earth that was created. In fact, the terms "created" or "creature," do not appear again in Genesis 1, until verses 21 and 20 respectively."[5.5]

This would also be consistent with the concept of beliefs regarding an Atlantis or Lemuria—at least in terms of *some* life forms being present at that time; (between Genesis 1:1 and 1:2; or between the words "*earth*" and "*without form and void*").

Those who scoff at this idea, generally claim ignorance of plate tectonics on the part of the proponents, as the reason for this belief.

However; although "evidence" regarding the timeframe is sketchy at best; *if* some type of continent such as Atlantis existed, it existed at a time between one million and one hundred million years ago—chronologically likely long before the *created* hosts and the kibosh (English) directive; and even longer before the *formation* of A & E. The "plates" can move substantially in one hundred million years. If something similar to Atlantis existed, it is generally believed to ultimately have become covered in water. If this sounds familiar to those who understand early Genesis, there are very good reasons for this familiarity.

So to those who might still maintain that the *creation* of the earth was a process extending far beyond the end of Genesis 1:1, the question becomes this: Why would God create an earth that required replenishment, and subduing, (putting the kibosh on), and dominating, and then refer to created man as hosts; which is a fighting force;

rather than creating an earth perfectly suitable for man? The simple answer is that He *wouldn't*; and He *didn't*.

Most agree that the Bible is primarily a book about redemption. But few understand what this actually means; i.e.; the actual *extent* of this redemption. It is generally, (erroneously), understood; that it is solely the redemption of man with which the Bible is concerned. However; the Bible is not merely concerned with the redemption of man, but also the redemption of the very earth itself—perhaps even the entire material ream.

This can easily be seen in the latter half of Genesis 1:2 and onward, where God begins to take redemptive action. Then the created hosts are advised to take redemptive action. Then likely through the formation of Adam, the seeds are sown for the Son to engage in the (immaterial) redemptive process; along with, and with assistance of the hosts.

It is also commonly believed that the redemption of man is an act of grace; i.e.; getting something that one does not deserve. Meaning; that despite man's "wicked and sinful ways," God nevertheless extends grace to man in providing "undeserved" redemption for that immaterial part of man.

If it is so stipulated that God *meant* it, when in Genesis 2:1 and elsewhere He referred to man as hosts; or in the original Hebrew:

"tsâbâ'; a mass of persons (or fig. things), espec. reg. organized for war (an army)"[5.6]

Then God would necessarily be the ultimate commanding officer of these hosts. And it is a fact that no commanding officer would ever consider rescuing his fighters as an act of grace, or any type of *undeserved* action. In fact, it is the *duty* of any commanding officer to rescue any and all of his fighters when reasonably possible.

In the case of *God's* hosts or tsâbâ', this situation is even more so. Man is brought into the world with no knowledge of his Divine purpose. Although some might try to argue that at some point that immaterial part of man volunteers for the job, with "informed consent;" there is no known evidence that would support this.

In addition, it is abundantly clear that even if this were so, any *information* part of any such "informed consent" is unavailable to most hosts most of the time. Thus hosts are simply thrown into a constant battle; with no knowledge of the enemy, or that he is even at war. And God himself knows, as stated in Romans 3:23, that all men sin.[5.7] Thus God knows that all hosts *required*, *require*, or *will require* redemption.

The test for *not* requiring redemption is 100% success in each and every battle, and that all, (except one), men fall short of this. It is simply not possible to win each and every battle; particularly when most or all the fighters do not even know they are in a redemptive war beyond themselves; or the true actual purpose for the same.

The purpose of redemption is salvation—whether it is the immaterial part of man, or the earth itself. Whether it is the ultimate salvation of man via the redemptive act of justification, or the redemption of the earth; redemption must always be paid for; if it is to be redemption (balanced). Else it would be theft, which would then be unbalanced.

The more specific purpose of these redemptions, is the restoration of former status; i.e.; it is a "salvage operation." With respect to man; this is the restoration of the former status of the immaterial part of man with respect to returning to its (original) source; despite the contaminations of sin sustained in battle. With respect to the earth; it is the restoration of the earth to what it was by design at the end of Genesis 1:1.

Man as a host, has known only the state of the earth as that which requires battle; but does not realize that he knows only this. Man is largely unaware of the condition of the earth *before* the changes caused by the enemy, which will ultimately be restored to the original state—at least according to "Revelation" and elsewhere. Thus man confuses this current *transitional* state of the earth, (constant battle); with the *original* and the *ultimate* state of the earth.

This is one reason why man often confuses the acts of the enemy with the acts of God. Man; not knowing that he is by design a *host*, and thus has no knowledge of his role as a *host*; simply does not and cannot understand why he must exist in such a *hostile* environment. Thinking that it is God who caused this hostile environment; man cannot reconcile the evil and wickedness currently present on the earth, with a kind and loving God— nevertheless he must. The result is a myriad of contrivances; most if not all of which cannot sustain or survive any serious level of scrutiny. If a premise is false; then barring a serendipitous event; that which is then derived from said premise, is likely to also be false.

All men sin. Nevertheless, there are *saints* and there are *sinners*. Saints *try not* to sin and fail. Sinners *try to* sin and succeed. Although the result, is that there are substantial differences in the *amount* of sin between saints and sinners; this is not the point. It is a matter of intention. And it is a *binary*; meaning that any thought or action, is either consistent with or inconsistent with the will of God. Thus those who choose sin, are choosing to act against the will of God; and therefore are necessarily choosing to act in furtherance of will of the enemy.

This, (choosing sin), is consistent with the viewpoint of the enemy. The enemy believes that God has supplanted his, (the enemy's), authority; and he, (the enemy), has been working for a very long time to "remedy" the situation.

A major problem for the enemy, is that his authority "peaked" at some time between Genesis 1:1 and 1:2. God began to intervene at some point in Genesis 1:2. God then *created* the tsâbâ' or the hosts, to "put the kibosh" on the earth. Meaning:

to replenish and redeem that which was redeemable by man, and only by man—even if the exercise of man's free will required divine assistance as a *means*; i.e.; *dunamis*, or *supernatural* power.

Much later on, God then *formed* from existing matter, he who would ultimately be called "Adam;" and then *fashioned* "Eve." This began the Hebrew, (one from the other side), bloodline, using the enemy, (as nâchâsh—the *hisser*),[5.8] in furtherance of His will.

God then introduced Messiah, Who in addition to providing salvation; both *lowered* the enemy's capabilities, and *raised* the available power of the hosts. [John 14:12 tells us: "*He that believeth on me, the works that I do shall he do also; and greater works than these shall he do; because I go unto my Father.*"[5.9]]

Thus; the slope of the graph of the enemy's capabilities has been consistently downward; while the slope of man's has been upward—whether realized by man or not. More about this later.

It matters little that the enemy believes that it is *he* who is the ultimate sovereign, and that statists believe that *they* are the ultimate sovereign. The commonality is that both believe that God is *not* the sovereign, and each acts accordingly.

One main difference is that unlike statists; the enemy knows full well that he is "*subject to God the Bible* (and) *natural law*;" but the enemy believes that this (his) "subjection" is merely a temporary condition. As seen in Job, the enemy in fact utilizes natural law to his advantage whenever he can.

Another main difference between the enemy and statists, is their respective views regarding H. Sapiens; AKA: the hosts, or tsâbâ'. The enemy is fully aware of the current and potential power of these "mass of persons;" and although he does not like it one bit, he understands it. The enemy also knows that except for supplanting God, he or it cannot change this hierarchy; i.e.; God, H. Sapiens, angels, then everything else; and again, he does not like it. The enemy knows full well what the results would be should he "get into it" with those in the aforementioned John 14:12; *if* any host or hosts truly understood what this passage means.

This is precisely why the enemy, through surrogates, has been trying to distort the meaning of the same; generally trying to substitute: "greater *numbers* of works" for: "greater *works*." He, (the enemy), has had enormous help in this from large portions of the religious communities, despite the fact that there is no factual basis whatsoever for this pretense. Keeping the hosts ignorant with respect to both their Divine purpose, and most particularly their latent power; is a high priority to him.

It seems that the statists are not so bright. As previously cited; unlike the enemy; statists believe that they are not "*subject to God the Bible natural law,*"—arguably merely because they say so. It cannot be left unsaid, that despite the fact that large parts of the end of the story have already been written, and the enemy loses; he nevertheless keeps on fighting. But even *he* knows that he is "*subject to God the Bible natural law*;" using it to his benefit whenever possible.

But statists do not in any way recognize the actualities of the hosts. Instead; they largely believe that hosts are equivalent to sheep, requiring statists to "lead" them. Statists do not recognize the true hierarchy. And they do not believe that all men are equal in this hierarchy— with the same changeable only by the consent of the hosts.

Rather; they believe in superiority of some over others *with respect to this hierarchy*. Statists do not believe in the power of the individual, but rather only the collective. Statists genuinely believe "you didn't build this;" because based upon their beliefs, they simply do not and *cannot* believe it possible, without their "help."

It is the absolute overwhelming desire of the enemy; whenever he is capable; to remove as many hosts as possible from the physical realm. He knows that any host who no longer physically exists, represents much less of a threat than a host who continues to physically exist. This is automatic, and a binary evaluation.

Statists however do not share this absolute vision. Instead; statists grade the importance of H. Sapiens according to an arcane system, based upon a host or group of hosts' perceived "relative value" to society. "Relative value" must be utilized here as this represents merely a *subjective* assessment by the statist(s). For example: A handgun manufacturer who develops a system to produce handguns at a lower cost; thereby freeing up citizen's funds for other purposes; has no positive value to a statist. Statists correctly view both the existence of, and the exercise, of 2nd amendment rights as a serious threat to their self-proclaimed sovereignty; which of course is quite true, and was provided as such by design.

Thus statists believe in a "sliding scale" with respect to the value of human life. This may at first *seem* to range from zero or even less, (a *burden* to society), for the presumed value of an unborn child; to maximum presumed value for either other statists; or those whom statists believe are necessary in order to maintain their "absolute sovereignty"—including and most especially *their* offspring. However the truth is far more heinous.

Any detailed discussion of abortion is far beyond the scope of this work. Nevertheless; a few observations are merited; as to the extent that one is a statist, one takes one position; and to the extent that one is not a statist, the opposite position is likely to be taken.

There is much in the issue of nomenclature. It is well known that there are those who are referred to as "pro-life;" and there are those who are known as "pro-choice." These arguable misnomers are designed to be socially acceptable, and each arguably represents a euphemism.

The term "pro-life," was selected based upon the assumption that an unborn child is in fact "alive." This assumption is based both upon emotional factors as well as "scientific evidence;" which is proffered as "proof."

If *this* were so; then "pro-choice" would be a misnomer, and should either be "pro-death" or "anti-life." "Pro-life" proponents tend to be more "religious;" with those of the "pro choice" persuasion tending to be less so.

The presumption that an unborn child is alive, is disputed by those on the "pro-choice" side. The best evidence for this, (not alive), position would be Genesis 2:7; but for some reason(s), it seems this is never proffered as any type of "proof" for the same. If *this* position, (fetus not alive), were true, then "pro-life" is a misnomer, and should be "anti-choice."

It is ironic that the "pro-lifers" tend to be more "religious;" and yet the best evidence *against* this position is contained in the Bible. Furthermore, with respect to abortion they are in fact "anti-choice;" when free will and balance are clearly God's will. The argument is that the unborn need protection, and there is much merit to this. But if the unborn child is not alive, this clearly represents interference with the free will of those adults who are in fact alive.

It is even more ironic that as stated, the "pro-choice" position best defense is contained in the Bible, but is never utilized by them. And if this were not such a serious matter, it would be also almost comical that the statists in this group proffer "pro-choice" with respect to abortion; but they are anti-choice anywhere else possible— including sometimes even the quantity of a soft drink that can be sold in one container.

Statists believe that H. Sapiens are generally incompetent, and require that "womb to the tomb" guidance and protection be provided by the collective; unless of course it happens to be an unborn child.

Chapter 6

Statism's Ultimate Objective

Earlier it was stated: "It seems that the statists are not so bright." This could be rephrased as: "It seems that the statists are not so smart." But although they themselves may not be so "smart," their actions and inactions are in fact quite "SMART."

Goals can be rather ethereal, such as: "I want to be obscenely rich." (More about this one later.) But what does this actually mean? What are the actual objective requirements for attaining the status of "obscenely rich," as opposed to "filthy rich," or just "plain rich?" There are none, as each of these represents a *subjective* determination.

Unlike goals, *objectives* tend to be much more specific, and must meet certain requirements in order to be considered as such.

The acronym "SMART," is often utilized as the requirements for a thing to be considered as a true objective. There are many different views of what each of the letters of this acronym represents. But Specific, Measurable, Achievable, Realistic, and Time constrained, represent fair definitions of each letter in this acronym; thus when taken together represent a fair definition of "objectives" *in-toto*.

Statists may not be so "smart" in terms of the truth or falsity of many things. However; their *objectives* surely meet this "SMART" criteria, despite the blatant falsity of any of their core beliefs and foundational assumptions. The same can be said of the *objectives* of communist China.

It was also earlier stated that statism ultimately leads to eugenics. As shocking as this may sound, this is the natural and unavoidable "progression" of statism. To statists, the value of an individual is not as God sees it, but rather is as determined by the statists, who believe they are: *"not subject to God the Bible natural law, or any other religion or ethical system."*

Few are unaware of at least some of the horrific actions of Hitler. What many do not realize, is that Hitler's actions were not some new idea solely as the result of one lunatic. Mao was responsible for the estimated deaths of upwards of seventy million. Stalin was likely responsible for the estimated deaths of upwards of fifty million, as once they were in contact with Western culture; they became contaminated, and *unredeemable*. These thus were so *deplorable*, as to be shot on sight when returning home, even if returning in victory.

George Bernard Shaw, a famous playwright, who lived until 1950 once stated:

> *"A part of eugenic politics would finally land us in an extensive use of the lethal chamber. A great many people would have to be put out of existence simply because it wastes other people's time to look after them."*[6.1]

It would be convenient to simply assume that this quote is extremely misleading, because it is taken out of context. The problems with this position, is that Shaw makes it quite clear that the subject of his statement is "eugenic politics," and not the criminal justice system.

Furthermore; he makes it clear that it is: "simply;" because it "wastes other peoples time to look after them;" that for this sole reason, these people "would have to be put out of existence."

If it is nevertheless somehow stipulated that Shaw was taken out of context, and he did not actually mean what it seems that he meant; the following quote, once again from George Bernard Shaw, would then require an inexplicable explanation:

> *"The notion that persons should be safe from extermination as long as they do not commit willful murder, or levy war against the Crown, or kidnap, or throw vitriol, is not only to limit social responsibility unnecessarily, and to*

*privilege the large range of intolerable
misconduct that lies outside them, but
to divert attention from the essential
justification for extermination, which is
always incorrigible social
incompatibility and nothing else."*[6.2]

Res ipsa loquitur—the thing speaks for itself.

There seems to be a bit of disagreement as to what constitutes *genocide,* vs. what constitutes *democide.* Genocide is technically killing or *murdering* those members of an entire *genus.* The genus *Homo* refers to all those classified in said genus, including *Sapiens* as well as other less developed and extinct beings.

More commonly, *genocide* actually refers to the killing or murdering of a large number of people, based upon some common characteristic other than genus. Genocide can take place as the result of state, (governmental), action; or non-state, (non-governmental), action.

For purposes of this discussion, *democide* refers to the killing or murdering of individuals or groups of individuals *by a government.* And this is not done as a penalty for criminal behavior, which actually injures another individual or society as a whole; such as the aforementioned: "*willful murder, or levy war against the Crown, or kidnap, or throw vitriol.*" But rather, here this, (democide), is done for other "crimes" such as the also aforementioned: "*incorrigible social incompatibility and nothing else.*"

The use of the term "incorrigible" by Shaw, merits some consideration. Although today many believe that "incorrigible" is often considered as synonymous with terms like unconscionable, unimaginable, despicable, etc.; back in the time when Shaw utilized *incorrigible*, this was not so. The better synonym for incorrigible would be "uncorrectable."

Shaw is or was not necessarily referring to the *nature* of the behavior; but rather its perceived "social compatibility," and "nothing else." This is confirmed by Shaw's delineating those acts which were commonly understood as punishable by the death penalty at that time. Clearly those stated crimes were already "socially incompatible" to the point where death was the penalty. Thus Shaw was referring to "socially incompatible" behaviors, that were well outside of those already proscribed by law.

Shaw's use of "incorrigible" meaning "uncorrectable," clearly implies that a decision must be made regarding the "correct-ability" or lack thereof; of certain traits or behaviors. (It must be asked if "irredeemable and deplorable" could "synonymically suffice" for incorrigible?) This also then requires some person or persons *outside of the legislature* to make this determination; otherwise said behaviors would already be included in the (criminal) group Shaw delineates at the beginning of this quote.

Shaw is stating among other things: "Do not feel safe from extermination, just because you do not violate the laws where the death penalty can be

101

invoked. Just because you do not violate them; nevertheless certain behaviors that represent *'social incompatibility and nothing else'* also warrant extermination."

Radical Islamic Terrorists hold this view, as any "religious" "social incompatibility" with their views of Islam warrants extermination. Hitler believed that those who were socially "incompatible;" such as Jews, Blacks and many more; warranted extermination. Stalin believed that once his troops were "contaminated" by exposure to the "west," they were socially "incompatible;" so they were met with machine gun fire as they exited the trains— again even if they were returning *victorious*.

But of course there is no way that any person in the United States of America could ever possibly be deprived of life by the government without the due process of law (democide). Any "just" death penalty would require violation of some law or laws where the death penalty was an option; and one either must confess to the crime; or be found guilty by a jury of his or her peers certified for the death penalty; and be lawfully sentenced to death by a judge. In the US, simply being alive could never under any circumstances be sufficient for a death sentence—right?

> *"One of the traditional methods of imposing statism or socialism on a people has been by way of medicine. It's very easy to disguise a medical program as a humanitarian project. Most people are a little reluctant to oppose anything*

> *that suggests medical care for people
> who possibly can't afford it."*[6.3]—
> Ronald Reagan 1961

Although this is often understandably vehemently disputed, the facts nevertheless remain pesky things. Irrespective of any euphemistic intentions; the Affordable Care Act, from the outset contained provisions for determining precisely who it is that would be permitted to obtain medical treatment, and who would not.

These so called "death panels;" however they otherwise may euphemistically be termed; do or in fact did exist, and utilize a process similar to QARY (quality adjusted remaining years). Meaning: that unelected bureaucrat(s), will determine who obtains or does not obtain medical treatment; including who lives or dies; based upon their assessment of the "value" of the remainder of that person's life. This is essentially the provision of a death penalty by omission; and is not based upon any act that a person may have engaged in; but rather upon what they are *perceived* to be— arguably the most heinous form of "identity politics."

In order to meet the threshold for a decision by said "death panel," it seems that an affirmative QARY decision would have already been made by a given patient and/or the patient's family. Had the *patient* and/or the *family* decided that the QARY was negative; i.e.; that such that no treatment was desired; then there would be nothing for these panels to decide.

Thus the actual *purpose* of this provision, is to have these unelected bureaucrats decide whether the *cost* of the proposed treatment is justified by their own QARY assessment.

If there were no such panels, then the recommended treatment would be performed. So the true purpose of these panels is to interfere with a patient obtaining recommended treatment, if the panel believes that the value of a patient is such that it is less than the cost of the treatment. [This is in contradistinction to *medical necessity*. True medical necessity, is based upon whether a given treatment is necessary for a given condition; and although the patient and/or the family might weigh this medical necessity; it and of itself, generally does not take into account either the cost of the treatment, or the "value" of; as opposed to "quality" of; the remainder of the patient's life.]

The question must be asked as to precisely what reference is utilized with regard to the value of a patient's life? Specifically it must be asked: value to whom? Surely the value is sufficient to the patient and the family—else the decision to not treat would have been made by *them*.

By Hobson's choice, it is the purported value of the patient *to society* that is being determined by these panels. Thus the situation is such that the life of a human being may be ended by *omission* of treatment, simply because of the *perceived* value of the life of this human to *society*—the wishes of the patient and the family notwithstanding.

This decision is to be made by these unelected bureaucrats, who were hired specifically to cut health care expenditures. This is done by said "panel" assigning a value to a human life, in order to determine if it is worth the health care expenditures. The main question being: Is said human's purported "value," less than the cost of the treatment required to preserve it?

If one combines portions of the two aforementioned Shaw quotes, we have:

> *"The notion that persons should be safe from extermination as long as they do not commit willful murder, or levy war against the Crown, or kidnap, or throw vitriol... A great many people would have to be put out of existence simply because it wastes other people's time to look after them."*

It matters little that Shaw is concerned with wasting "other people's time;" and or but; the Affordable Care Act is concerned with "wasting other people's money."

Neither does it matter, that those such as Shaw advocate *actions* which result in death; and the Affordable Care Act contains provisions that permit, (arguably require), *inactions* that result in death. In each case, individuals determine whether another person lives or dies based upon their perceived value to society, and not because of any criminal penalties.

Many opponents, (and even some proponents, including Harry Reid, Senate Majority Leader 2007 to 2015), of the Affordable Care act, believe that the same was designed to fail. Meaning; that the Act was not in any way primarily designed to provide affordable health insurance; with this purported purpose being merely an illusion or a ruse.

Rather; the primary purpose by design, was to insure that all private health insurance was destroyed, thereby requiring the introduction of a single payer system; i.e.; the Federal government.

And deliberately built into this system, was a means by which the desires of those such as Shaw could be fulfilled by means only slightly different than those utilized by Hitler, Mao, and Stalin. Irrespective of the *means*, the result is the same.

It matters little *how* the government engages in deprivation of life without due process. The willful withholding of life saving treatment against the wishes of the patient constitutes *murder*— irrespective of any proffered legislative or administrative authority.

In a civilized society, lives are not taken by the government, simply because of what a person is; and in the complete absence of any *mens rea* and *actus reus* causing injury to some party or parties. In civilized society, old age and/or infirmity alone can never meet this threshold. But here, the thinking is that being elderly or infirmed provide a contrived *mens rea* and *actus reus*; which causes injury to society, by forcing society to pay monies in order to sustain life.

It does not require a particularly high degree of cynicism to see how this could be utilized for political purposes. This would have seemed unimaginable until just a few years ago. But after the Internal Revenue Service's illegal treatment of conservative organizations without consequence or accountability, one should no longer feel safe "from extermination as long as they do not commit willful murder, or levy war against the Crown, or kidnap, or throw vitriol…"

The only safety from this would be for one to consistently not require any healthcare services— the more "economical" provision of the same, being the very purpose for which the Affordable Care Act was purportedly passed.

A single payer healthcare system is and always has been extremely important to statists, as once the government becomes the underwriter; the government then becomes able to take actions to minimize losses, including the aforementioned eugenics; on "behalf of the people." There is and always has been one main purpose for this; and that purpose is control.

Once it is determined that certain behaviors; or lack of behaviors; present the likelihood that this single payer will sustain a loss, then any such behaviors, (including remaining alive); or lack thereof; can simply be banned proactively. Non-healthcare private insurers have been doing this for some time. If one wants to insure a building, there are certain requirements imposed by the underwriter before insurance will be issued. One cannot maintain hazardous conditions or certain "attractive nuisances" on the property; and at the same time maintain insurance.

In the case of the government being the underwriter for health insurance, they, (the government), of course would have a similar interest in protection against any losses. Behaviors that might in the eyes of the bureaucrats in any way increase the likelihood of a payout, would simply be banned. And any person's *inactions*; such as not going to the gym; would not be permitted, with many types of action becoming mandatory.

This is what statism is always about. It is always about control; and as a "natural" progression, ultimately and particularly even control over who lives and who dies. Given all that is known to be true, there is no other possibility other than any statist who looks in the mirror, would see a frabjous image of the enemy himself.

It is always about control. This control is the antithesis of free will—no matter how well it may or may not be disguised. Often it is simply a matter of pride; e.g.; "because I say so" or "because I like or don't like it." It makes little difference as to the motive; unless there is a true *clear and present danger* involved.

Money and power are essentially interchangeable. The application of power can easily result in money; and the application of money can easily result in power.

Chapter 7

Dress Rehearsal

An extensive search of the internet; reveals that the "relative risk" of "ETS" or Environmental Tobacco Smoke, and/or "SHS" or Second Hand Smoke, at least according to the serious studies; can be liberally approximated to be at most about 130%. This includes individual studies, as well as the "meta-analyses." (A distinction should be made between ETS and SHS, because of the changes produced when tobacco smoke has been inhaled/exhaled; as opposed to environmental tobacco smoke.)

What does this mean? Most would interpret this to roughly mean an increased risk of physical disease, due to, (caused by), the presence of ETS and SHS, to be about 30%. However; this is not actually so. In order for a relative risk to be considered significant, most disease related organizations for many years required relative risks at a minimum to be 200% to 300%; with 200% required to even be considered as a *correlation*, (association), and 300% being required for *causation*. One simply cannot utilize a 30% figure for any meaningful assessment because of "confounding factors."

For example: It may be the case that in a smoker's home in a rural area, the windows are usually open; thus providing a source of fresh air. Therefore the actual harmful effect of ETS or SHS could actually be much *greater* than is reflected in the 30% figure.

Or it may be the case that the same occurred in an urban areas, where opening the windows brings in a steady stream of pollutants such as vehicle exhaust, brake dust, etc.; polluting the air in the home. Here the real culprit would not be ETS or SHS, but *external* pollutants. In this case, the contribution of ETS or SHS to actual harmful effects would actually be *much less* than the 30% figure would indicate; with the same at least partially being the result of contaminants unrelated to tobacco. This is why to any serious statistician; the 30% number is meaningless, and no statistically based conclusions are possible.

Thus the fair conclusion is that whether or not ETS or SHS poses any health risks whatsoever cannot currently be determined—it might, and it might not. The problem with this "ambivalence," is that some of these studies date back to the 1950's; and yet the highest possible increase in relative risk that has been obtained in over 60 years of studies is at the very most, (liberally construed in *favor* of health risks), about 30%. This does not guarantee a "null report," but it does make one wonder if another 60 years of studies would be likely to yield any different results.

The question at bar, is not whether ETS or SHS is annoying or odiferous. The question here is not whether EST or SHS necessitates frequent cleaning or repainting. The question is not whether smoking is a disgusting habit, and tends to give one halitosis. And the question here is most certainly not whether *statistically*, *smoking* (first hand), represents a health risk to the *smoker*. The question is whether ETS or SHS presents a health risk to *non-smokers*. And the honest answer, is that by the standards generally utilized for most if not all other health studies; this remains far from proven or even in any way statistically *correlated* in over 60 years of studies.

It cannot be overemphasized, that this information is *not* in any way provided to encourage the use of tobacco; or to in any way proffer any conclusions or comment regarding any potential health risks of ETS or SHS. Rather, it is the *process* that merits examination. What *is* being encouraged here is truth.

Is it possible that the government simply could have so much more knowledge and wisdom than that which is possessed by those who for decades utilized the 200% (correlation/association), and 300% (causation), standards for health risks? After all, there are some who call the police to get the "real truth" about what the upcoming storm will "really" be—as though the police have some source of information mere meteorologists lack. Namely; some type of inside *knowledge*;" and/or some unique police *authority* with regard to lawful storm severity.

The answer of course in both cases is no, in that government has no such greater knowledge or wisdom. The truth of course is that these ETS/SHS "conclusions," represent simply a matter of *control*; and are merely masquerading as health concerns, if it can be stipulated that the statistics should in any way matter.

It is interesting to note the *means* by which the government chose to "protect" non-smokers from these "health risks;" that as of this writing; have not even any proven correlation to, or any association with, either ETS or SHS.

It seems that the logical action, would have been to require air filtration, and establish clean air standards for areas where smoking is allowed; and some states, for certain circumstances, have done this, to some extent. But this does not fill the need, as this would not represent a means of *behavior control*, which of course is vital to statists. Rather, this would represent merely a *compensatory* mechanism, and allowing free will to continue. If clean air were the goal, this would be the best solution. If behavior control is the goal, then this simply will not suffice.

So the most popular method; is simply to make it a crime to smoke in any location over which the government has claimed jurisdiction to do so—as well as in many locations where they should not, and in actuality in fact do not, have any such jurisdiction for control. And even in states where the "clean air" approach is taken, there have also been *governmental* efforts to ban smoking in areas where it was previously permitted.

Although the air in these "no smoking permitted" venues might currently still "stink," and remain unhealthy from a myriad of *other* contaminants; at least here the free will of the smoker; (and many bar, bowling alley, and restaurant owners); can be controlled to the liking of those in power.

Since the figures regarding health hazards from ETS and SHS are statistically meaningless; what then was the rationale for these actions?

There are two distinct possibilities:

Firstly; the government may actually believe that it has "*much more knowledge and wisdom than that which is possessed by those who utilize the 200% (correlation), and 300% (causation), standards for health risks?*"

Or *secondly*; would be the "not take any chances" approach, in that since smoking is believed to statistically be a grave health risks to *smokers*; it likely then also must necessarily represent a risk to *non-smokers*—any and all meaningless statistics from 60+ years of studies regarding the latter notwithstanding.

After all; if history provides any guide; "even if it saves just one," provides sufficient justification for banning a previously legal activity for millions of citizens in areas where the government believes it can—no matter how unproven or miniscule the purported "risk."

So we are back to that pesky "equation:"

If It Saves Just One Life ≥ |Certain
Deprivation of Constitutional Rights|

It would be very easy to try and "plug in" the aforementioned liberally construed 30% increase in relative risk figure here in order to try and "balance" this equation. The problem; is that in a *statistical* sense, this 30% figure *does not exist.* Thus; *there is no statistical basis for the left side of this "equation" to have any value greater than zero.*

Certainly one could employ the "common knowledge," or "everybody knows," or "it just makes sense," approach in an attempt to obtain a value greater than zero for the left side; but this represents neither science nor statistics. And a strong argument exists that if any of these "arguments" were in any way true, 60 years of studies would have indicated such.

And since the right side of the equation is "absolute value" the *least* that it could ever be would be zero. Given the costs involved; both in terms of personal freedom, and in dollars in this undertaking; the value or quantity of the right side is far from zero. Many businesses such as the aforementioned bowling alleys, were forced to cease operations after the implementation of said smoking bans.

Nevertheless; based upon the government's actions, the same believes this: [If It Saves Just One Life ≥ |Certain Deprivation of Constitutional Rights|], is a valid equation and thus applies with respect to second hand smoke, and thus non-smokers. Here we are being told that zero is always greater than or equal to another number that must be greater than zero. But of course that that makes perfect sense and is perfectly acceptable—as long as one is not subject to natural law.

And as previously mentioned, even if it could somehow nevertheless be stipulated that SHS and ETS present health risks; the remedy that provides the maximum protection of rights, is or would be clean air standards. Smoking would be permitted, but areas where smoking is permitted must have filtration so that the air quality would be the same or better than non-smoking areas. But the problem with this approach of course, is that although this would eliminate the problem of any purported potential health risks, the problem of insufficient behavior control would remain.

It is interesting to note; that the government will not ban the use of *tobacco*; the same being the very substance involved with *smokers*. This could easily be justified merely by utilizing the statistical results of studies that have in fact for decades, shown clear and convincing *correlation* and more than arguably *causation* for serious health risks. Yet; it will ban and has banned smoking in any area that it can, based upon studies that show to date no such correlation or causation for health risks to *non-smokers*.

It is also interesting to note, that at the same time the use of tobacco is being restricted; the legal "recreational," (non-medicinal), use of marijuana is expanding. The only place smoking is allowed in a commercial aircraft is in the cockpit, because nicotine increases mental acuity. The same, (increased mental acuity), cannot even be argued regarding the THC contained in marijuana.

So with regard to banning the actual *substance* used by actual *smokers*:

"If It Saves Just One Life ≥ |Certain Deprivation of Constitutional Rights|;"

is now admitted by the government
to <u>not</u> be a valid "equation."

In the case of ETS, (environmental tobacco smoke), and SHS, (second hand smoke), even where there is no demonstrated statistically significant risk to non-smokers; the government nevertheless purports to believe that this equation is valid, and bans smoking everywhere it can.

But here; with regard to actual, (first hand), smoke; where the statistics demonstrate a *significant* value, (avoided risk), on the left hand side of this "equation;" the government does not act to ban the substance.

According to Benjamin Fearnow, in an article titled "Study: *Third-Hand Smoke Exposure As Deadly As Smoking,*" dated 3 February 2014:

> "Cigarette smoking causes an
> estimated 440,000 deaths each year in
> the U.S., which is about one-in-five
> deaths. The CDC notes that smoking

causes more deaths annually than
HIV, illegal drug use, alcohol use,
motor vehicle injuries and firearm-
related incidents. . . (and that)
Secondhand smoke *causes* an
estimated 46,000 premature deaths
from heart disease each year in the
United States among non-smokers."[7.1]
(italics supplied)

Thus according to Mr. Fearnow, (it is assumed
that this is his true name), smoking kills, ("causes"
death), 440K people per year; with another 46K
that the SHS and ETS studies seem to have
somehow missed for over 60 years, that are also
being killed, ("causes" death), from *heart disease
alone* due to SHS.

Mr. Fearnow does not attempt to claim how
many others are "caused" to die from diseases
other than "heart disease," because of SHS. But
what he did claim; represents nearly half a million
deaths per year in the US alone—and arguably
many more if "SHS related diseases" other than
cardiac were to be considered.

Mr. Fearnow also claims that deaths from
smoking are more than "illegal drug use." One
might reasonable ask the reason(s) for making
"illegal drugs" illegal in the first place? If tobacco
causes more deaths than "illegal drugs" as he
stated; it seems that society would be better served
if the "illegal drugs" were made legal, and instead it
was tobacco that was banned. Or even better; keep
the "illegal drugs" illegal; and also ban tobacco. Yet

anyone who purports banning tobacco is not even taken seriously.

By Hobson's choice, the only logical reason that the government will not ban the use of tobacco, would be because of the tax revenues—federal, state and local.

In 2010, the Democrat House and Democrat Senate passed, and the Democrat President signed into law; the PACT (Prevent All Cigarette Trafficking) act; essentially making the internet sale of tobacco products illegal. This was done primarily so that tax revenues to states with confiscatory tobacco taxes could be maintained. Prior to this, tobacco products could be purchased online; either from retailers in states without confiscatory taxes, or from Native American lands. So the Federal government chose to willfully interfere with free trade, in order to keep these tax dollars flowing to the states.

No reasonable person would characterize the purchase of flowers or candy via the internet as "trafficking;" and be in favor of the enactment of legislation to prohibit the same. This is likely because any "sin" taxes on these items are negligible, and the larger retailers generally collect appropriate sales tax.

So when it comes to tobacco tax revenues ($), we have yet another "equation:"

Collection of Tax $ ≥ If It Saves Just One Life

In fact, if Mr. Fearnow is correct; here then the value of the tax revenue dollars is necessarily greater than the "value" of a *half a million lives per year*. Ergo: money is more important than lives.

This is easily illustrated by the death of Eric Garner in New York, who was killed in an altercation with the "cigarette tax" police, over the sale of "Loosies;" i.e.; loose (unpackaged) cigarettes. This purported "crime" was purportedly committed in avoidance of New York's confiscatory cigarette taxes. Mr. Garner's death in the "hands" of police; was reportedly the result of questionable police actions, and pre-existing health issues.

It must be remembered:

> *"Tobacco addiction sinks its claws in deeply, it's just as powerful of [sic] an addiction as heroin or crack cocaine..."*[7.2]—Al Gore

When someone invents an internet, his words should be taken seriously. To the extent that Mr. Gore may be correct, the government is taking full advantage of what in economics is referred to as an "inelastic" commodity. The "elasticity" of a commodity relates to how a change in price will affect the "quantity demanded." When a commodity is *elastic*, a significant increase in price will cause a significant decrease in the quantity demanded—depending on the degree of elasticity. When a commodity is *inelastic*, an increase in price will have little effect on the quantity demanded.

Our various governments obviously believe that what JFK said in his inaugural address: "shall pay any price, bear any burden, meet any hardship..." clearly applies to smokers. No matter how much governments raise the confiscatory tobacco taxes, smokers; believed to be under the influence of something "just as powerful of [sic] an addiction as heroin or crack cocaine;" will of course pay the taxes. And so when market forces come into play, the governments then conspire to "willfully interfere with free trade in order to keep these tax dollars flowing to the states." And there is a least one unarmed man dead at the hands of police because of this conspiracy. Any purported degree of "legality" of this death; does not make him any less dead. Any "If It Saves Just One Life" test apparently did not apply to Mr. Garner.

It must be asked what level of cruelty is involved in deliberately causing a smoker whose addiction is believed by those in power to be: "just as powerful of [sic] an addiction as heroin or crack cocaine...;" to be forced into "withdrawal" should he be onboard a commercial aircraft, (unless he "sneaks a smoke" with the captain); or should she decide to go to the local bar?

If the airline, or the owner of said bar wished to prohibit smoking; that of course had always clearly been their prerogative, and market forces would have been in play. Smoking is not and never was a guaranteed right in any, (someone else's), privately owned establishment. However; neither should the rights of said private owner be abridged with regard to the use of a legal substance by patrons.

And even if statistically significant evidence regarding any harmful effects of STS or ETS were available; at what point does the government have the "just" authority to intervene in this way and manner? If a bar owner wishes to allow smoking in his establishment, that should be his or her decision. If "clean air" were the issue, the government should have taken the "clean air" approach. This would satisfy all those who are concerned with health, but of course would be highly unsatisfactory to those whose prime interest is control. The "boundaries" seem merely to be what many of those in the government believe they can "get away with;" AKA: "pull off."

Because of the misrepresentations, (euphemistically stated), of the health risks of SHS and ETS, smokers have been become an underclass, believing that their habit harms their fellow men, and have substantial guilt because of this.

And as previously mentioned; there is now the issue of third hand smoke as per the inclusion of the same in the above referenced title: "*Third-Hand Smoke Exposure As Deadly As Smoking.*"

Polycyclic aromatic hydrocarbons are believed to be one of the major culprit(s) for the increase health risks associated with "Third Hand Smoke." The idea seems to be that these compounds which are contained in tobacco smoke, are deposited upon dust particles and surfaces in areas where smoking is permitted, and are then "picked up," by non-smokers causing health risks: "*As Deadly As Smoking*"—at least according to Mr. Fearnow.

According to the National Cancer Institute (NCI), these PAHs (polycyclic aromatic hydrocarbons) are "*mutagenic—that is, they cause changes in DNA that may increase the risk of cancer;*" and according to NCI, are in fact contained in cigarette smoke. However also according to NCI, polycyclic aromatic hydrocarbons, are also "*formed when fat and juices from meat grilled directly over an open fire drip onto the fire causing flames. These flames contain PAHs that then adhere to the to the surface of the meat.*"[7.3]

To the extent that these health risk concerns associated with "third hand smoke" are valid, there seems to be another serious and much larger public health risk. These polycyclic aromatic hydrocarbons, (PAHs), are being produced continuously for about twelve hours per day or more at each and every steak house, every flame broiled hamburger facility, and anywhere meat is cooked over an open flame. This includes each and every time a homeowner "fires up the grill" that has open flames, and then cooks any type of meat.

Thus those who work in these facilities, are being exposed to these "mutagenic" substances at very close range for extended periods of time. Others in and around these facilities, are likewise being exposed to these "mutagenic" substances. And to the extent that the health risk concerns associated with "third hand smoke" are valid, the same rules should then apply with regard to these health risks.

In fact; due to the greater *concentrations*; any health risks associated with these compounds that are found in cigarette smoke, (according to the NCI); would likely also be much greater with meat cooked over an open flame. In addition; via the very same purported "third hand smoke" mechanism, these "mutagenic" substances are being released into the atmosphere where they can likewise attach to dust particles, and cling to surfaces and people at distances far from the source. It is likely that if one can smell this smoke, one is being exposed at some level. However it cannot be said that if the concentration is below that level which would trigger an "odor," that the air is "safe."

This sounds a bit like radioactive "fallout," with respect to the detonation of "surface burst" nuclear weapons. It is quite fortunate for all, that neither tobacco nor food contains any radioactive substances.

"Wait a minute! What about Polonium-210? It is "common knowledge" that cigarette smoke contains some level of radioactive Polonium-210— the same being that which is believed to have been the cause of the poisoning death of Putin's foe, Alexander Litvinenko.

And is it not so, that the tobacco companies were accused of all sorts of conspiracies regarding failing to disclose these facts? It was and is believed by many, that the source of the PO-210 was the fertilizer that was being utilized to nourish the tobacco plants.

According to a study published July 1983 by Oak Ridge National Laboratory (ORNL/TM-8831), for the Florida Institute of Phosphate Research: "*Food ingestion also represents the major source of naturally occurring PO-210 intake. Additional data collected by Spencer and her colleagues (1977) indicates that 77.3% of an adult male's daily PO-210 intake is supplied by food, 4.7% by water and 0.6% from air. Inhalation of cigarette smoke provides more PO-210 (17.1%) than drinking water and air combined."* The study further states: *"The overwhelming source of plant PO-210 is the deposition of its precursor, PB-210, on plant surfaces during rainfall events."*[7.4]

Thus according to this study, 82.6% of a male smoker's intake of PO-210 is from food, water, and air, with *"primary* cigarette smoke" being responsible for 17.1%. This adds up to 99.7%, thus it seems the study had some "rounding issues." It also seems that the real culprit for the inclusion of PO-210 is rainwater, at the "bottom" of the food chain.

Nevertheless, the "Abstract" at the beginning of this study states: *"For the majority of internal organs evaluated, the dose resulting from smoking commercially available tobacco products is comparable to or greater than the dose estimates for ingestion of naturally occurring dietary PB-210 and PO-210."*[7.5]

This type of folderol is often seen in the "conclusions" of SHS and ETS studies. The numerical results presented in a study will have little or no statistical significance whatsoever. Yet the author of the "conclusion," and subsequent "recommendations;" will nevertheless bloviate about the dangers of SHS and ETS, recommending that some sort of action should be undertaken, based upon these statistically insignificant results—arguably relying on the fact that this "conclusion," is all that will be read or understood.

Here with the Oak Ridge report, at least the author presents enough qualifications; i.e.; "wiggle room;" to render the conclusion of the statement meaningless and therefore useless, if read as written.

In this "abstract," the author is first concerned with *organ deposition*, and not *dose* or *ingestion*: "*For the majority of internal organs evaluated,*" He then concludes with a comparison between said organ deposition and *estimated* dose for ingestion: "*is comparable to or greater than the dose estimates for ingestion of naturally occurring dietary PB-210 and PO-210*"

PAHs, and PO-210 to some extent seem to be part of life. One can choose to smoke; (primary); and arguably increase one's intake of PAHs (as well as some others such as tobacco specific nitrosamines of which little seems to be known); and also increase PO-210 intake perhaps about 17.1%. And/or one can also choose certain food products, and achieve a similar or even greater result.

However the germane issues here are not about health risks to smokers, but rather health risks to non-smokers. With regard to the same, it seems that these alleged "third hand smoke" culprits would have contributed to statistical findings in SHS or ETS to some extent. Yet as of this writing, no statistically significant findings can be found that SHS, ETS, or "third hand smoke" presents a statistically proven health risk to non-smokers—at least according to commonly used parameters. There is a plethora of opinion, but a paucity of statistical fact.

Even if in the "exercise of extreme caution," or the "just in case" approach, one wished to minimize exposure to any and all pollutants, the air filtration approach is the better answer; and except perhaps for the initial cost, this is inarguable. But this approach is unacceptable to the statists, because it maintains personal freedom, and market forces. This is about control, and the ability to cause massive changes in socially acceptable behavior with little or no scientific foundation.

The truth; the concerns of genuine liberals notwithstanding; is that the war on tobacco represented a "test run" for something else with much greater social implications.

Ergo; the real issue has nothing to do with tobacco, smoking or health concerns; but rather the ability to cause massive societal changes with at most little, or no evidence.

Chapter 8

Showtime

Pollution is a relative term, in the sense that it can be *qualitative* or *quantitative*; and it can be *material* or *immaterial*.   Pollution is derived from the Latin: "*polluere* 'to soil, defile contaminate...*"[8.1]

Although this root may arguably seem to necessarily then be, or in fact should be the root for *politics*; it nevertheless appears that this is not so, as *politics* is believed to be of Greek origin.

Qualitative pollution can be considered to simply be the *presence* of something that should not be present. In this sense it is a contaminant.

Quantitative pollution can be considered as the increase in the *quantity* of something that *should* normally be present; but is present in amounts *greater* than that which is believed to be appropriate.

Qualitative pollution is a binary; in that the contaminant simply should not be present in *any* quantity. *Quantitative* pollution is much more subjective, in that it is not the presence of something; but rather the *amount*, *quantity*, or *concentration* of something that is the issue.

For example: there are certain substances that should not be present in any quantity in drinking water. If said substances are present in any amount, (qualitative), this is then considered polluted water as it contains contaminants. Other substances are considered to be acceptable at determined levels, and when present in drinking water, *at* or *below* these levels, water is not considered as polluted. The problem with *quantitative* pollution; is that the determination of the levels of acceptability are often prone to *error*.

The above represent *material* pollution for obvious reasons. However there is also *immaterial* pollution. "Fake news," or what for decades was referred to as "disinformation," is one example of immaterial pollution; with the falsity representing the contaminant.

However, in certain senses; just as in material pollution; it can be either qualitative or quantitative. "Information" which indicates that 2 + 2 = 3 is *qualitative* pollution; because the sum of these numbers can be easily proven to not equal 3. Information which in instead of being provable, is considered to be true because of some consensus of minds; can be considered as *quantitative* pollution, in that the *quantity* of individuals that believe a thing in no way contributes to veracity. And history is replete with instances that prove this is so.

The previous analysis of "second hand smoke" and "environmental tobacco smoke," represents the analysis of a blend of truth and disinformation.

SHS/ETS is *qualitative* pollution, in that at least some of the components of tobacco smoke should not normally be present in air that is considered to be non-contaminated.

But it is also *quantitative* in that in a backwards sense, the purported health risks are considered to exist because of deliberately misinterpreted statistics. Meaning: that in order for these health risks to be considered as a truth, the *standards* for correlation/association and/or causation had to be lowered, and in fact were lowered significantly; (from the requirement of 200% - 300% RR or relative risk, to at most 30% RR); in order to obtain the desired result. This is equivalent to predicting with certainty a landslide election win, when the polls are well within the margin of error.

And it is clear that many in government want smokers to continue to purchase cigarettes for tax revenues, (and "tobacco settlement" monies); but at the same time making it as difficult as possible for smokers to smoke. This of course is inconsistent with both natural law and common sense.

But there are two classes of individuals involved in this:

One group, (true liberals), genuinely believes the governmental usurpation and other actions undertaken, are justified in the interests of public health.

The other group (statists), celebrates the victory for two main reasons:

Firstly, is merely the issue of control. Why was smoking chosen for this control? Because one can only control what one can control. After 9/11, there were pleas from "famous people," encouraging individuals to go to NYC and patronize restaurants, as many were in trouble financially. At the very same time, NYC was in the process of banning smoking in these same restaurants.

The *second* and greater reason; was to *prove* success in the utilization of statistically meaningless statistics for the purposes of massive societal behavioral changes.

———————————

Weather is a "short term" phenomenon, varying day by day. In fact; "quasi-tautologically" speaking; it can be said that *"weather changes like the weather."*

Climate is measured on a much longer basis, arguably 20-30 years or much longer. And climate is and has been changing. *"Panta Rhei;"* usually attributed to Heraclitus; means *everything flows*.

Long Island NY, is a terminal moraine. Like a bulldozer backing up and leaving the debris in front of the blade, Long Island was formed by glacial retreatment. This means that the climate was substantially colder prior to the retreating, and warmer at the time any retreating began, and thereafter.

It is also a certainty, that man affects global temperature. The body heat generated by the existence of just one man necessarily changes the temperature of the earth—irrespective of the magnitude of this change. Likewise; the mere lighting of just one match will produce some thermal increase. Thus in an absolute sense, any and all activities of man will affect the temperature of the earth.

The real question is the significance of the activities of man *in-toto*; and whether or not said activities represent a significant factor with respect to current changes in climate. Meaning: what is the Δ or difference in how the climate *is* changing including man's activities; as compared to how it *would* have changed in the absence of man? This Δ or difference would then represent man's contribution to climate change.

As in the case of "second hand smoke" or "environmental tobacco smoke," no attempts are being made here to express any opinion regarding this controversial matter. Rather, it here again is the *process* that merits consideration.

At the outset, it must be noted that what is now considered "climate change," was quite recently referred to as "global warming." Given that one primary consideration with respect to climate is generally temperature, it should be asked *why* the need for this change in nomenclature? Why is it that what once was known as "global warming," is now known as "climate change?"

The term "global warming," generally represents both a *cause* and an *effect*. As an *effect*, "global warming" itself is purportedly the *result* of man's activities. Man's activities create heat in the ecosystem; thereby being the *cause* of an increase in global temperature; i.e.; global warming. And "global warming" is purported to be a *cause* of ice melting, sea levels rising, and a myriad of other changes.

"Global warming" is specific with respect to polarity, even if non-specific with respect to magnitude. Meaning; that this term indicates that the temperature of the earth is *increasing*, even if the *magnitude* of any such increase cannot accurately be determined. One of the reasons that the magnitude cannot be accurately determined, is because of the location of the temperature sensing equipment. Temperature sensors that were once placed in remote areas which would produce the most accurate measurements of ambient temperature; can now be found in macadam covered parking lots—the same areas glider pilots seek for "lift."

But it seems reasonable that any "global warming" would not be "season specific." Any increase in *global* temperature would be just that; and not exacerbate and remit depending upon the current season of any given geographical area. After all, it is *global*; and while summers are in full bloom in the Southern hemisphere producing purportedly record high temperatures; areas in the

Northern hemisphere can be simultaneously experiencing record setting brutal winter temperatures. This represents a change in both magnitude *and* polarity. This should not be so, if the earth or "globe" were merely warming.

These aberrations of a true "warming" trend, are presented as though increased molecular motion somehow "knows" when it is summer and winter. This reminds one of the "joke" about the man who bought a thermos. When he was asked how he liked it he replied: "It keeps coffee hot, and iced tea cold. How does it know?" Thus to suggest that the cause for these paradoxical temperatures is "global warming," provides an insufficient, and arguably oxymoronic explanation.

Enter the term "climate change." Unlike the term "global warming;" the term "climate change" provides the means by which a *non-specific* explanation for changes in both polarity *and* magnitude can be utilized.

> Q: "How can the winters be so brutal when there is global warming?"

> A: "Those brutal winters are not because the globe is *warming*, that's silly. It is because the climate is *changing* man, don't you know that?"

Here this unspecified "changing," provides the "explanation" for the paradox. The summers are hotter, and the winters are colder, because the climate is *changing*. The "cause" of both the harsh winters and the brutally hot summers, is the "changing" climate. This may bring to mind the previously cited quote from Karl Popper: "*A theory that explains everything, explains nothing.*"

In addition to the obvious, there are some other problems:

Carbon dioxide (CO_2) is colorless and odorless, and is gaseous at the temperatures in which man exists. It is exhaled by many life forms including human beings, and is *required* for photosynthesis by plant life.

According to the *EPA*, CO_2 represented 81% of: "Greenhouse Gas Emissions" in 2014;[8.2] while *NASA* claims that water vapor is: "The most abundant greenhouse gas."[8.3] Perhaps this apparent discrepancy can be reconciled, if water vapor is not considered as "emitted." Thus according to the EPA and NASA, the top two culprits in climate change is a substance that is exhaled by humans and *required* by plant life; and the vapor of a substance that covers approximately two thirds of the planet.

And also according to the EPA, "... GHGs (greenhouse gases) act like a blanket, making Earth warmer than it would otherwise be. This process is commonly known as 'greenhouse effect.'"[8.4]

On this very same page, the EPA displays a graph illustrating the peaks and valleys of CO_2 concentrations and Antarctic temperature change, reasonably coinciding for the past 800,000 years.[8.5]

The peak seems to be about 300 ppmv (parts per million by volume), occurring about 340,000 years ago; with 260 ppmv noted about 600,000 years ago.[8.6]

On NASA's website, as of this writing, CO_2 current concentration is 405.6 ppm; stating: "Carbon dioxide levels in the air are at their highest in 650,000 years."[8.7]

NASA explains that: "The Earth's climate has changed throughout history;" and "there have been seven cycles of glacial advance and retreat;" and that "Most of these climate changes are attributed to very small variations in Earth's orbit that change the amount of solar energy our planet receives"[8.8]

The EPA explains that: "Over the last several hundred thousand years, CO_2 levels varied in tandem with the glacial cycles. During warm "interglacial" periods, CO_2 levels were higher. The heating or cooling of earth's surface and oceans can cause changes in the natural sources and sinks of these gasses, and thus change greenhouse gas concentrations in the atmosphere.[2] These changing concentrations are thought to have acted as a positive feedback, amplifying the temperature changes caused by long-term shifts in Earth's orbit. [2]"[8.9] The use of "thought to have acted" should not be overlooked. (Citation notes of "2" is deliberately left in.)

Thus it seems that according to both the EPA and NASA, "climate change" would actually be better termed "global warming;" as it is "making Earth warmer than it would otherwise be," that seems to be causing all of the purported problems.

[It must be noted that at the time of publication, the EPA website now shows: *"This page is being updated. Thank you for your interest in this topic. We are currently updating our website to reflect EPA's priorities under the leadership of President Trump and Administrator Pruitt. If you're looking for an archived version of this page, you can find it on the January 19 snapshot;"*[8.10] when these referenced pages are now attempted to be accessed]

The logic of the purported process is difficult to follow. If simply for the purpose of analysis, the presented data is stipulated to be true; then over the past 650,000 years there have been at least 7 (seven) episodes of the climate changing. And that "Most of these climate changes are attributed to very small variations in Earth's orbit that change the amount of solar energy our planet receives;" (NASA); or that "temperature changes (are) caused by long-term shifts in Earth's orbit." (EPA)

It must be asked with respect to each of these previous episodes of temperature increases, wherein was the source of the CO_2? Since either man did not exist in significant numbers; or if he did, there is no evidence of any significant direct or indirect "biological" emissions" of CO_2. Perhaps it was the dinosaurs? The same providing green house gases to "act like a blanket, making Earth warmer than it would otherwise be;" (EPA) and thereby also "thought to have acted as a positive feedback, amplifying the temperature changes caused by long-term shifts in Earth's orbit."

Assuming this is all true, the same merely represents the explanation of a mechanism whereby when the temperature of the earth increased *initially* due strictly to "orbital" changes, with the natural *resultant* increase in CO_2 via release from "sinks" contributing to *further* temperature increases.

For 650,000 years the earth has been warming and cooling with CO_2 levels rising and falling accordingly; with the proponents of "climate change" readily admitting that the rise in CO_2 was the *result*, and not the primary cause of the primary temperature increase—with perhaps the increased CO_2 levels only providing a secondary "blanket" effect. But with the current purported "climate change" theories, it seems the reverse is true.

Today it is believed that what was historically the *secondary result* of temperature increase, (natural release of CO_2); is now the *primary cause* of the temperature increases. At first blush, it may seem that "the sun rising increases temperature," has now become "increases in temperature makes the sun rise."

The only current "rational" explanation for today's "climate change," is that it is solely this "blanket effect" of the CO_2 that is the culprit. Man made greenhouse gases such as CO_2, and water vapor; are providing this "blanket," and not allowing heat to escape.

It is also unclear how any such effects are *apportioned* with respect to CO_2 and water vapor. Since as stated, water covers approximately two thirds of the earth, this represents a rather large "sink;" but a major problem for the "climate change" proponents, is that companies that actually *manufacture* water, are not particularly easy to find.

But any such "blanket," would in actuality also represent an insulator. Although today it is believed that this blanket is preventing the escape of heat; forty years or so ago, this blanket; (along with other types of pollution); was believed to be *blocking* the energy of the sun, and severe global *cooling* was predicted.

But as Col. Tom Parker was known to say: "Figures don't lie." Here it can be said that *data* doesn't lie—assuming of course, that the data itself is not a lie.

The source of the above "data" presented by the EPA as cited by the EPA's aforementioned footnote "2" is: "*Climate Change 2013: The Physical Science Basis. Contribution of Working Group I to the Fifth Assessment Report of the Intergovernmental Panel on Climate Change.*"[8.11]

According to the Intergovernmental Panel on Climate Change's (IPCC's) website, the IPCC "*was established by the United Nations Environment Programme (UNEP) and the World Meteorological Organization (WMO) in 1988...*"[8.12]

It is unclear why the EPA chose to cite data from an *intergovernmental* panel, (IPCC), established by the United Nations; rather than citing data from recognized individual American scientists.

It seems that Forbes magazine has had some issues with this IPCC. In an article titled: "*The IPCC's Latest Report Deliberately Excludes And Misrepresents Important Climate Science*" dated 31 March, 2014 states:

> *"Like its (IPCC'S) past reports, this one
> (Working Group II Contribution to the
> Fifth Assessment Report) predicts
> apocalyptic consequences if mankind
> fails to give the UN the power to tax
> and regulate fossil fuels and subsidize
> and mandate the use of alternative
> fuels."*[8.13]

The "past"report that Forbes is referencing, that this particular report, (Working Group II), is "like;" appears to be the very same "report," (Working Group I), the same cited by the EPA as *their* source, via the aforementioned footnote "2."

The Forbes article goes on to compare the IPCC's report, with another report released the same date as the article, the same being the "Nongovernmental International Panel on Climate Change; (NIPCC); founded by atmospheric physicist S. Fred Singer. Eight specific points, ("reasons for concern"), that are made by the *IPCC*, are addressed by the *NIPCC* in said report.[8.14]

Following are excerpts from NIPCC regarding these eight IPCC points:

> —"...Climate change ranks well below
> other contributors, such as dikes and
> levee construction, to increased
> flooding....
> —"...Rising temperatures and
> atmospheric CO_2 levels play a key
> role in the realization of such (rising
> agricultural) benefits...

—"No changes in precipitation patterns, snow, monsoons, or river flow that might be considered harmful to human well-being or plants or wildlife have been observed that could be attributed to rising CO_2 levels. What changes have been observed tend to be beneficial.

—"...Continued atmospheric CO_2 enrichment should prove to be a huge benefit to plants by directly enhancing their growth rates and water use efficiencies...

—"There is no support for the model-based projection that precipitation in a warming world becomes more variable and intense. In fact, some observational data suggest just the opposite, and provide support for the proposition that precipitation responds more to cyclical variations in solar activity

—"Rising temperatures and atmospheric CO_2 levels do not pose a significant threat to aquatic life...

—"...Multiple lines of evidence indicate animal species are adapting, and in some cases evolving, to cope with climate change of the modern era...

—"A modest warming of the planet will result in a net reduction of human mortality from temperature-related events. More lives are saved by global warming via the amelioration of cold-related deaths than those lost under excessive heat..."[8.15]

There clearly seems to be substantial controversy regarding what was at one time "global warming," and is now referred to as "climate change;" notwithstanding the fact that it is often stated by "climate change" proponents, that: "the science is settled." The fact is that it does not in any way appear that the "science" is in any way "settled." In fact it is unclear that there is even any science involved—irrespective of whether "settled" or "unsettled."

"Climate change" proponents, often state that somewhere between 97% and 99% of the world's scientists agree with "climate change."

It is unclear if these figures represent scientists who believe that it is true that the climate is changing; or scientists who believe that that which the proponents state about "climate change" is true. There is a difference; and that difference is precisely what is man's contribution, if any; as well as what—if anything—can or should be done about it?

"Climate change deniers" are those who disagree with purported "causes" proffered by the "climate change" proponents; but most do not necessarily believe that the climate is not changing. One can agree with the idea that the climate is changing, and at the same time disagree with "climate change." It is interesting to note the use of the term "deniers."

A fair antonym of "denier" is "believer." Thus those proponents of "climate change" can reasonably be self-characterized as "believers;" by their own usage of the term "denier." This is fair.

Precisely what is a "believer?" If one has four apples, and then gives two away, how does one then characterize the subsequent actuality of the fact that two apples remain? When asked: "How many apples remain?;" would the usual response be: "I believe that two apples remain.?" More likely the response would be: "Two apples remain;" or just "Two."

Generally, the use of "believe," represents a qualifier to the purported "answer." Without the use of "believe" as a qualifier, the answer would be based upon the *knowledge* of the actuality. With the use of this qualifier, the answer is not based upon the knowledge of the actuality. In fact with the use of this qualifier, the question is in fact not even in any way answered.

The "apple" inquiry was about an actuality. But with the use of the qualifier "believe" in the answer; this represents information not about the subject of apples, but rather shifts to information *about the person asked*. "*My reality*, about the *actuality*, is that two apples remain.," would be another way to rephrase this answer.

The term "believer" is often associated with religion. In many religions, "belief" constitutes the affirmation of a *reality* for purported actualities; when the evidence for the existence of the *actualities* is below that which is normally considered as reasonably self-evident. Solipsists correctly believe that all one knows for certain, is that the solipsist exists; i.e.; "I am."

Thus in order to discuss anything else, requires that *assumptions* be made. One such assumption, would be that *something* in addition to one's "I am" exists—else there would be nothing else to discuss. Another necessary assumption, would be that *another* "I am" exists—else there would be no entity with which to discuss the product of the first assumption.

In normal every day life, levels of evidence for the existence of actualities are generally presumed to be based upon "common sense"—even if the term "common sense" is considered as oxymoronic by some. Unless some assumptions about the existence of actualities are made based upon commonly accepted levels of evidence, nothing would ever be able to happen. Sometimes; as in the case of a mirage; these levels fall short.

This is seen with the legal levels of proof, ranging from: "probable cause," through "preponderance of evidence," through "clear and convincing evidence," and "proof beyond a reasonable doubt." And generally; the more severe that the legal penalty is; the higher the level of proof that is required.

And sometimes a "mirage" occurs, where the incorrect decision is made. This is one reason why the *severity* of a penalty, is proportional to the "certainty" of the evidence required; i.e.; requires more "certain" evidence. "Probable cause" may allow limited interference with one's rights; but "proof beyond a reasonable doubt" is generally required for the penalties of incarceration or death.

When levels of proof are such that the evidence for the existence of an actuality falls below that which is "normally" considered as "sufficient;" the term "believe" is often incorporated. When one "knows in his heart of hearts," this may be overwhelming *subjective* evidence; but falls short of the level of *objective* evidence required by others. Hence here; unlike as is the case with counting apples; statements regarding *belief* are appropriate.

"Climate change" *believers* are correctly termed as such. This is not to say that they cannot serendipitously be correct in their conclusions; but rather that the evidence thus far does not reach the "normally" accepted level to justify this conclusion.

The truth is that given all the considerations, "climate change" could best be characterized as a *religion*, rather than anything related to science.

Hence the *unintentional* self-characterization of the proponents of "climate change" as "believers;" by their *intentional* characterization of those who disagree with their beliefs as "deniers."

And in fact, it is interesting to note the methods utilized by these "believers," with respect to those who disagree. These methods resemble those utilized by religious zealots, rather than those normally utilized by proponents of science.

On 25 May 2016, five US Senators found it necessary to send a correspondence to US Attorney General Loretta Lynch, stating:

"We write today to demand that the Department of Justice (DOJ) immediately cease its ongoing use of law enforcement resources to stifle private debate on one of the most controversial public issues of our time—climate change... As you well know, initiating criminal prosecution for a private entity's opinion on climate change is a blatant violation of the First Amendment and an abuse of power that rises to the level of prosecutorial misconduct... As the US Court of Appeals for the Sixth Circuit reminded the Justice Department just weeks ago, 'no citizen—Republican or Democrat, socialist or libertarian—should be targeted or even have to fear being targeted' on the basis of ideological disagreement with the government."[8.16]

Once it became the practice to permit *thoughts* to be an aggravating factor in the determination of the "heinousness" of a crime, actions such as those attempted by AG Lynch were predictable.

It remains unclear precisely how the level of harm sustained by a victim of a criminal act, is increased because of the thoughts or beliefs of the perpetrator. Thus the "logic" behind so called "hate crimes;" where the penalty for a crime is greater than that for the identical crime; if and when the perpetrator *thought* or *believed* certain things; "set the stage" for this. It does not require much to expand the concept that if thoughts or beliefs can be an element of a "hate crime," said thoughts and beliefs alone can be civilly or criminally actionable.

Unfortunately; the only ultimate judicial protection against "thought crimes," would be the very same body that somewhat recently told us that if a law's provision was a tax, they could not hear the case until the tax went into effect. They then agreed to "hear it"—arguably constituting an admission that said provision was not a tax. But then ultimately ruled that it was a tax, and instead of postponing their decision; ruled that because of this, this same provision was constitutional, because it was a tax.

The reasons that "climate change" has become so political, is twofold:

Firstly; the proponents of "climate change," simply have fallen short of maintaining accepted scientific standards. There are issues of lost data, the locations of monitoring equipment, extrapolation of data and much more. Thus any conclusions or predictions based upon such non-scientific data and methods, is essentially without any scientific merit. This does not necessarily mean that what the proponents of "climate change" purport is false. It merely means that their views have in no way been scientifically determined; i.e.; "you can't get there from here."

Secondly; are the actual solutions offered for this purported problem. It is true that there have been substantial regulatory efforts to reduce CO_2

emissions in the US, and these have overall been quite successful—as long as the definition of "success" does not consider economic costs. Nevertheless, the consistent primary "solution" to "climate change," remains the transfer of enormous amounts of wealth—particularly to other countries. This is precisely why the EPA relies upon data from a creation of the United Nations, and not the "Nongovernmental International Panel on Climate Change; (NIPCC);" founded by atmospheric physicist S. Fred Singer, who is an American.

Thus although "climate change" is proffered as a crisis, whether serendipitously true or not; in its current form, "climate change" in fact represents merely a *means* to accomplish something else. And that *something else*, is the statist's dream—the massive international redistribution of wealth.

Rahm Emanuel, formerly President Obama's chief of staff, said it well:

> "You never let a serious crisis go to waste. And what I mean by that it's an opportunity to do things you think you could not do before."[8.17]

The similarities between the "second hand smoke/environmental tobacco smoke movement," and the "climate change movement," are striking.

The numerical results contained in the SHS/ETS studies and metanalyses are what they are. It is not the data that is in any way suspect, at least in the serious studies. The *atypical statistical significance,* (no acronyms please), attributed to these results is where the fabrication of the relationship between SHS/ETS and health risks is found.

The "trick" was to by some means form a cause-effect relationship using data that would be otherwise considered well within the margin of error in any scientific study or poll. Again; the *threshold* parameters for health risks had to be lowered from 200%-300% Relative Risk, to a 130% Relative Risk, in order for this relationship to be established.

The proponents had to be reasonably certain that the public would understand these purported *conclusions*; but either not look at, or not understand the *means* by which the purported "relationship" was achieved. If the true lack of any statistical relationship between SHS/ETS and health issues were understood; the public would never have accepted the schizoid behavioral changes imposed on them. "Schizoid," as citizens are now supposed to purchase tobacco products for the tax revenues; but at the same time be prohibited from using them in any area where the government believes it can prohibit said utilization.

The SHS/ETS actions in certain but many senses represented merely a trial run. If this sophistry, (the fatal flaw here being the *data* in no way supporting the conclusion), could be successful; (AKA: "pulled off"); then this behavioral modification, (manipulations), achieved would be dwarfed by the behavior modification possibilities with "climate change." Thus this would twice provide the aforementioned: "opportunity to do things you think you could not do before."

But with "climate change," the approach was to be a bit more bold. With the overwhelming success of SHS/ETS scheme, that attached extreme statistical significance to what in any other circumstance would have been totally insignificant data; (i.e.; a null report); proponents were emboldened. And in a sense, this approach would be much "safer" than the SHS/ETS scheme. This is because the fatal flaw would be contained in the *data* itself; which of course would be much more difficult for the "common man" to dispute. There is always that reliable: "You are not a scientist!" attack.

The possibilities for success in behavior modification, (manipulation), via a substance that human beings normally *exhale*, and plants *require*, are enormous—arguably limitless. Even *breathing* could ultimately be subject to governmental regulation. What better argument could exist for limiting human reproduction; eugenics/euthanasia and/or the establishment of requirements for massive reforestation and plant minimums.

But again, one must ask if where this seemingly limitless desire for control originates, is in fact where it appears to originate?

Chapter 9

A Thing That Is—

There is that which is; and there is that which is not. This seemingly sophomoric statement is often forgotten by many; and it represents the very antithesis of the statist's "creed."

Again, for the purposes of analysis, *actuality* is what currently *exists* or what *is*. *Reality* is that which is *believed* to exist, based upon perception and other factors. The process of an *actuality* becoming a *reality* is called *realization*. The *reality* of a true mirage includes water; but the *actuality* of a mirage includes no water. To *actualize* something is to bring something from the thought process; (quasi-reality); to a current actuality. No actuality can ever be 100% accurately perceived, thus reality always falls short.

Under *normal* circumstances, one perceives some portion of that which exists. The *reality* of a thing is *caused* by some degree of perception of the

151

actuality. It is true that there can be false perceptions such as the aforementioned mirage; or a movie, (which all involved usually know the "true actuality"); but the reality is the *result* of some type of actuality. Something exists and is perceived, and even if perceived incompletely, or erroneously; (e.g.; the mirage); the actuality *produces* a reality through perception.

As stated; one can ultimately produce an actuality through a reality, (actualization); but not just by the existence of the reality alone—at least when confined to the material realm. *Imagination* is similar to a reality, but with the subjective knowledge or belief that the thing does not yet exist. *Recollection* is also similar to a reality, but with the subjective knowledge or belief that the thing may no longer exist.

Unless the immaterial realm is involved, the existence of a reality alone will not bring into existence an actuality; neither will it cause any changes in an existing actuality. Although a reality can change based upon actuality; an actuality will in no way exist or change, simply and solely because of the existence of a reality—again at least when confined to the material realm. An actuality represents *that which is*.

But statists believe that actuality is determined by their reality, and not the reverse. Said belief, in and of itself, represents prime example of "*that which is not*."

This statist belief forms the basis for that which was previously cited:

A Thing That Is—

> *"A statist government treats its*
> *political sovereignty as a platform*
> *for moral sovereignty.*
> *In other words, as ultimate sovereign,*
> *the state is therefore not subject to*
> *God the Bible natural law, or any*
> *other religion or ethical system.*
> *A statist government need not be*
> *accountable to its own citizens."*

Thus this entire statist position, is based upon, and is an outgrowth of, *that which is not.*

Most H. Sapiens live and act according to their realities; which are supposed to be consistent with actualities—at least when mental sanity is present. When reality and actuality become *inconsistent*; most realize, whether this is pleasant or not, that it is their *reality* that is at fault; and the same must change to be in accord with the actuality. Most sane people would not expect to quench thirst from a mirage.

Statists live and act based upon their reality that what is so, is so; simply because they *believe* it to be so. When reality and actuality become inconsistent to a statist, it is the *actuality* that is at fault; and must change to be in accord with their reality.

The problem with this approach; is that in order to have change in an actuality, there must be some type of *cause*, for which the *result* is the change in the actuality. Huck and Tom "lettin on that there are pirates in the cave," represents insufficient cause to produce the actuality of "pirates."

This is part of the reason why statists are overly but genuinely concerned with the way something is presented. Statists genuinely believe that an actuality that is unpopular; would somehow become popular, if it could only be "explained better." This is because in their view, actuality is determined by reality; and that the actuality itself will somehow change and become popular, if a different reality can be achieved by a better explanation—e.g.; "We need to use different words."

This must be distinguished from lying. Statists lie all of the time, but here genuinely believe this reality/actuality – cause/effect relationship; whether they know they believe this or not.

Ayn Rand is attributed with stating:

> *"You can ignore reality, but you can't ignore the consequences of ignoring reality"*[9.1]—Ayn Rand

Here Ms. Rand uses the term "reality" in the more common usage. For more *specific* usages, reality and actuality are not synonymous, as previously explained. Reality is what we "know" as the result of perception; and in the absence of certain types of chemical substances, is almost by definition impossible to ignore. At the risk of appearing as a philosophunculist, if the word *reality* is replaced with the word *actuality*, the statement now would read:

A Thing That Is—

"You can an ignore actuality, but you can't ignore the consequences of ignoring an actuality"

If a woman becomes pregnant, that is an actuality; and normally something is going to happen in around nine months, no matter what anyone believes, recognizes, or ignores. This actuality can be ignored; but the consequences of ignoring this actuality cannot, (forever), be ignored.

It must be noted however, that statists do not in fact willfully *ignore* actuality. But since to a statist, actuality is "reality dependent," the same effect often occurs. Dealing with enemies with a reality based upon what you *believe*, *hope*, or *wish* they are or should be; despite overwhelming evidence to the contrary; (definition of delusional); can be quite disastrous. The same can be said of solving social issues or anything else. The actuality of the results of a response from "a thing," will be based upon what the thing is, (actuality); and not based upon what the thing is *believed* to be, (reality).

When a yes or no question is asked, the response is a binary. It can reasonably be stated that if *yes* is the correct response, then this represents an admission that whatever the subject of the question is, *exists*. If *no* is the correct response, this is then equivalent to stating that it *does not exist*. Even in the case of falsehood, the *admission* remains the same,

Whether one is discussing the "Big Bang," or discussing Genesis 1:1; one is necessarily discussing

155

different parts of the same actuality—whether *realized* or not. The "Big Bang" is concerned with the bringing into existence of time, space, and matter; and Genesis 1:1 is concerned with precisely the same thing. The difference; is that science is primarily concerned with the "physical" *cause* or *mechanism* of the phenomenon itself; and Genesis 1:1 is primarily concerned with the immaterial cause, and the "*caus*(er)." The "Big Bang" is what would have been witnessed, had there been an observer to the very events described in Genesis 1:1.

Each is concerned with two related entities:

First is the *primum movens*, or the prime mover. This is the effect with no cause; or that which existed *prior* to and subsequently created time, space and matter; i.e.; the *material* realm.

And it necessarily follows, that said *primum movens*, (Biblical God), could not have been in a realm prior to that realm's creation; which proves the existence of another realm without time, space or matter.

It also follows that prior to the creation of time, space, and matter, this *primum movens* must have existed in order to cause it; but the same could not have had any beginning, as there was not yet the existence of time. Although this is difficult to *perceive*; this nevertheless remains a logical requirement.

Secondly is the *process*. The "Big Bang" confirms that matter was brought into existence from non-matter. Likewise, that which is in Genesis 1:1 and is translated as "created," is the Hebrew word *bârâ*, which essentially means to bring into existence from nothing (no-thing). This is the primary source of confusion regarding the conflict between science and the Bible, with regard to the age of the earth, as previously discussed.

The original human beings, (as were the "heavens and the earth")," were *created* via *bârâ*—described as such utilizing this very same Hebrew word. But Adam was not created or brought into existence via *bârâ*, but rather was formed or *yâtsar*. And we are told precisely what type of matter or "thing" was utilized in forming Adam. Said matter, (yes-the thing exists), was *'âphâr*, generally translated as "dust."

It can be positively ascertained Biblically, that Adam was *formed* less than 10,000 years ago. But the *creation* of the original humans was way long before Adam, likely hundreds of thousands of years ago—the Bible does not say. [The detailed litigation and reconciliation of this confusion can be found in *"MeekRaker Beginnings. . ."*]

That which *created*, created that which was created. That which *created*, did *not* create that which was *not* created. And that which *created*, created that which came from the creator; and had to be that which was contained in the creator prior to creating. If that which creates is considered as a set; all that is created is necessarily a subset of that which creates.

This leads to what is likely the most paradoxical matter in the entire Bible—the *origin* of the source of "interference." Any difficulties, (and there are many), in understanding the Christian Trinity are dwarfed by this. It is clear that the recognition of the existence of an "opposing force" crosses the boundaries of religions, with the major religions all thus recognizing the existence of an *enemy*.

He or it is an *enemy* with respect to man; but merely an *adversary* with respect to God, which is how and why "Satan" is generally translated as *adversary*. The enemy can be involved with actions and inactions that result in man's physical death, (enemy); but this will not work with God—no matter what he, (the enemy), may think. Said enemy is known as: *Mara* in Buddhism, *Kali* in Hinduism, *Iblis* in Islam; and *Satan*, *devil*, and many other names in Judeo-Christianity. But neither the *origin* of said enemy, nor the *structure* of said enemy, is even remotely understood.

The Bible itself contains relatively little about the *origins* of enemy, and much of what *is* there is often grossly misunderstood. This information may have originally been contained in the Bible, but removed or modified over millennia. Thus the enemy is often only known by the *perception* of his or its "fruits;" the actualities of which will generally result in realities that are either seriously exaggerated, or seriously diminished. This leads to massive speculation about the same; much of which is often either self-contradictory, or contradicts with much of that which is known, or generally believed to be so.

Some believe that God created the enemy, in order for man to per-fect himself. But *how* or *why* could or would the Creator deliberately create less than perfect beings? *How* is it that a perfect being could create man in His "image and likeness;" and yet have the same require assistance to become perfect? In order to maintain this belief, one must then also believe that God either did not create man in His "image and likeness," and the Bible is untrue; or God Himself is not a perfect being.

And it must be asked precisely *how* God, who is a perfect being, here representing the "set;" could impart characteristics to a subset that are not contained in God's original set? It was not that way in what is commonly called Eden. Not only was there no "evil;" but there was not even so much as the *knowledge* of evil in Eden, or in the minds of the "residents" of Eden, until it was "imported" into the area. And the same question could be asked regarding the "idea" of God creating the enemy itself; i.e.: "Precisely where was it, that that which is of the enemy originated?"

A "power set" is all of the possible subsets of a set, including the null set and the set itself; and is derived by raising 2 to the power of the number of elements in the set. For example: the "power set" of a set with 2 elements, (A and B), is 2^2 or 4 possible subsets. The same being A, B, AB and {} or the null, empty, or void set. Thus although subsets can range from nothing to the full set itself, there is no possibility of the inclusion into a subset; any elements not contained in the original set. Therefore; in order for God to have created the enemy, God himself; here being the "*set;*" God would necessarily had to have contained the elements that formed the subset known as the enemy.

The standard argument against this would be: "God is omnipotent, He can do anything." Again, this is not actually true.

The correct statement is: "God can do anything that can be done." Meaning; that God cannot establish the rules that permeate the universe; and then arbitrarily violate these rules without providing a balancing factor.

Neither can God act in a manner that is both *consistent* with His will, and *inconsistent* with His will, simultaneously, regarding the same matter. In fact it must be asked, how it is that God is at any time capable of acting against His will?

Ergo; the enemy was *not* provided by God as a means for man to per-fect himself; and man was in fact created in the image and likeness of God.

The truth; is that it is the result of *exposure* to the enemy 24/7, that requires man to improve himself, (and also require salvation). It is also true that through the process known as *karma* by some; and $F = MA$ with equal and opposite reactions by others; "learning" can and does occur.

But what possible need would or could there be for that which is created in the "image and likeness" of God, to attain perfection while remaining just as created? The enemy is in one sense similar to an attorney "creating the controversy," which then requires his services to resolve. The difference is that with respect to the enemy, resolution can only be achieved by going *against* his, (the enemy's), thoughts, ideas, and suggestions.

As previously indicated: "*God can do anything that can be done.*" "Anything that can be done," does not include bringing a man into existence by *creating* him from *nothing*; and simultaneously bringing the very same man into existence at the very same time by *forming* him out of *something*. Believing that the story of Adam represents merely a more detailed recapitulation of the creation of the original hosts, *requires* that something that cannot be so, is yet somehow nevertheless so. There is no actuality that can include utilizing mutually exclusive; (the occurrence of one precludes the occurrence of the other); methods to bring into existence the same man at the same time.

The same can be said about the creation of the earth:

> "But from here on, things becomes somewhat problematic. In the very first two verses of the very first book, something else of great significance seems to have happened. As it reads, God no sooner created the earth and it appears that the earth was "formless and void,"... "

> "There are several possible interpretations of this "formless (some translations are "without form") and void." The easiest being that this refers to the contents of or on the earth. The earth was created, but there was nothing on the earth that was created.

It was completely void, *and* formless. Void meaning containing nothing (nothing); and formless meaning essentially the same thing; "less any forms." This may seem reasonable, although perhaps a bit redundant. Another interpretation of course being; that this means that the earth was somehow without form, in the sense of not being the oblate spheroid it is today, or any other recognizable shape.

"Many, if not most, believe that this state (without form and void) of the earth represents a transitional state between nothingness and the creation of the earth; as though for some reason, an omnipotent God had to create the earth in stages. The state of the earth at this time is often referred to as "chaos.""...

"This theory seems to be stating that "the earth" which was created, was in fact not earth at all; but rather some sort of "pre-earth mass," (authors' terminology), which for some reason is simply referred to as "earth" in the beginning of Genesis; but the actual earth not being created until afterwards. This theory also then necessarily requires that God would be the author or the creator of chaos.

"Earth, Mars, Venus etc. are all planets. In order to be considered a planet, certain criteria must be met; criteria which in the opinion of some, the former planet Pluto, as of this writing, no longer satisfies. Pluto is thus no longer considered a planet. The term "planet" means wanderer, as that is how they appeared to move in the sky with respect to the stars that appeared relatively fixed in their individual movements. When we have planets, we call them planets, and usually by name. When we have asteroid belts, comets, stars, or black holes; we call them such, because they are not planets, but something else. In our solar system, the asteroid belt is called such, because a belt of space debris is not considered a planet.

"Neither do we need, nor did we need to know the nature of the surface of a planet; nor what forms might exist upon it, to call it a planet. But to be considered a planet, which earth clearly is, it must have form, and thus cannot be without form. Whether or not any forms exist *on* said planet, or what the same may be, is irrelevant in general with respect to the planet designation; and is irrelevant specifically with respect to the earth.

"Now one might ask why God would create chaos, when He was trying to create the earth; and His Word clearly states that He succeeded? There is also a second question that necessarily arises: If God had created the earth in stages, why would it be necessary for us to know that the earth was created in stages? It would have been one thing if God merely created the earth this way, but it is an entirely different thing for Him to make sure that we *knew* that the earth was created this way. . .

"It seems reasonable; that in the beginning, God created the heavens and the earth just as the book states, and not chaos or a deep or a pre-earth mass. Then something happened which made the earth without form (or formless) and void; that after all being the way it reads. Most translations and versions do not actually state "*and then*," but that is the only explanation that seems to make any degree of sense. Although it must be stated, that the *Interlinear* version, on *Scripture4all.org*, does include in their translation: "she (the earth) became.""[9A9.2] [Excerpt from "*MeekRaker Beginnings. . .*" Reprinted by permission]

This becomes a bit more interesting; in that again, the actual word *created* in Genesis 1:1 is in fact the aforementioned *bârâ*; so this can only mean the bringing into existence from *nothing*. Thus the conclusion of Genesis 1:1 tells us what it was that was created; or brought into existence from nothing—the same being the earth. Any changes or other actions undertaken with respect to the product of *bârâ*; i.e.; the earth; could no longer be considered *bârâ*. This confusion is similar to the confusion regarding the aforementioned *created* hosts, and the *formed* Adam.

If it can be stipulated that Genesis 1:1 is true as written; then the heavens and the earth were created, (Big Bang), during the time period of Genesis 1:1 or the "Beginning;" with said "Beginning" concluding at the end of Genesis 1:1.

From Genesis 1:2 onward, this represents what took place, an unspecified time long ago; but took place *after* the conclusion of the "Beginning," when the earth was actually created.

What the earth became; "without form and void;" then necessarily happened long *after* the creation of the earth. These changes, representing *effects*, then necessarily required a *cause*. The source of the cause had to be either God, or not God.

A fair read of God's actions after the "without form and void" condition described in Genesis 1:2; clearly show that He was not content with the "without form and void" status. Thus for it to have been God that caused these changes, and then acted to restore the original status; He would then have necessarily changed His mind twice. Firstly He "created the heavens and the earth." He then would have had to have acted in order to establish the "without form and void" status which the completed earth *became*. And He then would have had to have acted in a manner to begin to restore the original, or some other status of the earth. Of course this is nonsensical.

A revisiting of Revelation 12: 7-9 is warranted here:

"And there was war in heaven,
Michael and his angels waging
war with the dragon.
The dragon and his angels
waged war,

and they were not strong enough,
and there was no longer a place
found for them in heaven.

And the great dragon was thrown
down, the serpent of old who is called
the devil and Satan, who deceives
the whole world;
he was thrown down to the earth,
and his angels were thrown
down with him."[9.3]

"A fair read of Revelation Chapter 12 *in-toto*, is that it is chronologically "all over the place." This is not surprising. As previously discussed, John was permitted to enter the immaterial realm where there is no time. He then wrote what he recollected without any type of time reference for all or most of what he had witnessed.

"But clearly Revelation 12:7-9 refers to a time when Satan was still in heaven. Although a bit scant on details, it does show us what happened; and what was the result. Likely it was his expulsion; and his subsequent appearance while he was being thrown down to the earth, being the source from which the name Lucifer was derived...

"There are some mixed tenses contained in this passage from Revelation. Most of it is in the past tense; but the "is called the devil" and "deceives the whole world" are stated in the present tense. Thus it seems fair to assume that the events recounted in the past tense are historical; and those stated in the present tense are current events

"We are told that Satan was thrown down to the earth along with his angels, because there was "no longer a place found for them" in heaven. But precisely when did this event occur? Unfortunately, it does not state the timeframe, but what we do know is that the earth must have existed prior to his shall we say, departure; as we are told that earth was his ultimate destination; whether by anyone's intention or not."[9.4] [Excerpt from "*MeekRaker Beginnings. . .*" Reprinted by permission]

As previously addressed, some might argue that all passages in Revelation refer strictly to the future. And also as previously stated, this is not so. In fact it is unclear that *any* time distinctions could be made in the timeless realm. Furthermore; this, (future only position), would require that either there are two Satans; or that he was somehow returned to the immaterial realm pending his reappearance at some future time. Even man has no such luxury without salvation/justification.

"It is likely more accurate to say that Satan was ejected from the immaterial realm, and thus thrust, at least partially, into the material realm; with earth as either the only possible destination; or perhaps merely the closest destination at that time. If so, then this presents a significant problem for him, because the life forms on earth were designed to exist in the material realm; but Satan was not.

"This could mean that although Satan once resided in a realm where he had immense powers as an angel; at some point he became subject to at least *some* of the rules or limitations of the material realm. Perhaps this is why Peter tells us that: "Your adversary, the devil, prowls around like a roaring lion, seeking someone to devour."[9B] There is clearly a consideration of space, (prowling around); as well as time, (seeking). It is true that part of Peter's statement may be read as a simile, but that would relate to the similarities to a roaring lion, and not necessarily the devil's actions. Or, and more likely; Peter is attempting to describe a phenomenon for which no correct word exists; thus a description using the word "like" to indicate the closest similarity is intended, rather than an actual comparison.

"If it is assumed that devour means consumption of whatever is the object of the "seeking," then one might fairly ask why any animal would warn it's prey with roaring; prior to killing it for food? This would seem to substantially decrease the likelihood of success; or at a minimum, cause more effort to be required. If devour just means to destroy; to kill when it is not to be used for food; then likewise why would it make any sense to warn the prey?

"But what if Peter really meant that the prowling and roaring constitutes the first effort in his seeking; is in a sense similar to radar? In the use of radar, a signal is first sent or transmitted; and then the returned signal is examined in order to gain information; "stealth" aircraft being specifically designed to minimize this returned signal. In a likewise manner, the enemy "roars;" here actually meaning those "thoughts ideas and suggestions" humans get into their heads; often knowing not from whence they came. He then watches one's reaction in order to determine their specific potential level of "devourability." His goal being to "get our attention" as he did with "the woman," so that he can get a foothold with which to continue the process. Thus, he does not like it when it is the case where little or no signal is returned; meaning that he has been largely or completely ignored."[9.5] [Excerpt from "MeekRaker Beginnings. . ." Reprinted by permission]

It is understood that much of what has been stated, and what logically must follow; may be quite controversial to many. Nevertheless the Word tells us what it tells us.

The problem with *understanding* the Word, is the predictable result of doing essentially what the Supreme Court of the United States is and has been doing for decades. That is: referring not back to the original document, but rather utilizing what *men* have said about the *meaning* of the document—there the US Constitution. This leads to generational errors, depending upon the number of "layers" of "truths" upon which the current "truth" is based. Opinions of the Constitution change, but the actual Constitution and its true meaning remain unchanged—except by amendment. The same can be said about the original Bible both in Hebrew and Greek—but here there is no *legitimate* means of amendment.

For the same reason, understanding the Word has been subject to the same problem. Many believe that Genesis 1:2 is in no way as described here, but rather a description of God "perfecting" the earth after He created it. Of course this makes no sense logically, because not only are we told that the creation of the earth was completed at the end of Genesis 1:1; but it must be asked why God would create an imperfect earth? The only possible answers are that he either did not *want* to, (would not), create a perfect (already perfected) earth; or that he *could* not create a perfect earth.

It must again be asked wherein lies the "subset" of *imperfection* contained in the "set," (that which is of God); that is known as God? *How* is it that a perfect God *could* create imperfection, much less why *would* He?

It must again be remembered that true creation or bârâ, is the bringing into material existence something from nothing. Here it must again be emphasized that "nothing" refers to "no thing" contained in the material realm. This is not a substitute for a "causeless effect." There is a *cause* for the results of bârâ, but that cause is found in the immaterial realm; most *particularly* prior to the existence of the "other" or "material" realm. Once *modifications* are made to anything existing in the material realm, irrespective of where lies the cause for said modification, this can no longer be bârâ.

Genesis 1:1 essentially contains three components: the *cause* or acting party, a description of the *action*, and the *result*. God was the cause; *bârâ* was the action; and the bringing into existence the material realm, (the heavens and the earth), was the result.

We are *not* told in Genesis 1:1, that God formed the heavens and/or the earth from 'âphâr, (often translated as "dust" in the *formation* of Adam).

Neither are we told that He created anything else that would require "perfecting," nor are any other modifications contained in subsequent verses, in order to make the end of Genesis 1:1 to "eventually" become true. The end of Genesis 1:1 represents the end of the "Beginning;" with all subsequent actions *after* the earth was completed. Thus the *need* for such actions was the *result* of another *cause,* said cause being provided by an entity other than God.

"God's ways are mysterious," is often proffered as the reason that there must be some sort of third explanation—one that man simply cannot comprehend. The fact is that although "impossible to comprehend" may in fact be the case when trying to comprehend things such as the immaterial realm, (*heaven* but not the *heavens*); and its relationship to the material realm. But this is *not* the case in comprehending creation in Genesis 1:1, and what happened afterward; as we are *told* what happened, despite any gross misunderstandings of the same.

The aforementioned reliance upon experts, rather than the Word itself; is a major factor in this lack of understanding, and subsequent "excuse making" for the same. Often there are *emotional* factors affecting *intellectual* "facts," and their *understanding.* Although this in itself is understandable, nevertheless knowing and understanding the facts trumps emotional concerns every time—if it is *knowledge* and *understanding* that is truly desired.

One example is the translated term "day," when describing God's actions after Genesis 1:1. This is proffered as evidence as part of the "timing" of the "perfecting" process, which is measured in various translations as: "days." Thus it is believed that God acted on these separate "days." The Hebrew word *yom* or *yôwm* is this word, commonly translated here as "day."[9.6] However, *yom* can refer to a 24 hour day, or the light portion of the same as we commonly know it; or it can refer to the completion of a season or a process.

If used as a measure of *time*, this is analogous to the Greek word *krono*—"chronometer," currently in use as a "hi-tech" term for a clock. If used as the description of a *process* completion; this is analogous to the Greek word chiros—chiro referring to *hand*, as in the *hand of God*. [*Chiropractic* literally means: "easily done by hand."]

Since the luminaries did not exist until the third or possibly the fourth day, depending upon how it is read; it must necessarily be asked precisely how it was or by what specific mechanism it was that at least the first two days were measured? However, if *yom* refers to the *process*, rather than the 24 hour day or the light portion of a day, this all begins to make sense.

The timeframe seems to be as follows:

—≈4,500,000,000 BC

God created the heavens and the earth. This is commonly "scientifically" referred to as the "*Big Bang*." As previously stated, many believe this to not be so; because the subsequent redemptive actions taken after Genesis 1:1, are instead erroneously considered to represent merely a more detailed explanation of the events of Genesis 1:1.

The process of the creation of the heavens and the earth actually ends at the conclusion of Genesis 1:1, with the word "earth." This represents the conclusion of the "Beginning;" with all that happened afterward happening at a time neither in the "Beginning," nor as any part of the "Beginning;" but at some unspecified time *after* the conclusion of the "Beginning."

—Some unspecified time after 4,500,000,000 BC

The enemy was "thrown down" to the earth—banished from the *immaterial* realm, and thrust *partially* into the other, or *material* realm; to a "place," which was the *neither* or *nether* "world." The conditions of the earth then *became* those as described from Genesis 1:2 onward, ("without form and void"). There is no reliable Biblical information available as to *when* this happened.

At some unspecified time, God began to intervene and reverse some of the changes to the earth, in order to restore it to a more desirable and original status. This can be referred to as the "beginning" of the *redemption* of the earth.

God then again engaged in the *creative* process, but to a much more limited extent than in Genesis 1:1. However; the redemption of the earth was not *to be* completed by God himself, and in fact was not completed by God himself; and remains yet uncompleted to this very day.

It must be asked *why* it was that the redemption of the earth was not completed by God Himself, and instead He created "hosts" for the kibosh(ing)? After all, God is omnipotent, so why did He choose to only partially redeem the earth? There seems to be only one answer that makes any degree of sense.

As previously stated, God can only do that which *can* be done. In order to have any just or balanced action, both *power* and *authority* are required (see ěxŏusia (Greek)).

It is indisputable that an omnipotent being has the power. Ergo: God must have not had the authority. Clearly God had both the *power* and the *authority* to create the heavens and the earth in the first place. So would it be in any way reasonable to believe that He nevertheless somehow lacked the authority to *redeem* the earth *in-toto?*

This question is best answered by asking another question. Why was it that God did not *prevent* the destructive changes to the earth, (cause), with the results, (effect), as described in Genesis 1:2 and onward in the first place—thus removing any possibility of an earth that for untold years, would require "kiboshing?"

Meaning; that although He clearly had both the power and authority to *create* the heavens and the earth; He nevertheless somehow lacked both the power *and* authority to stop all of the destruction caused by the enemy after the enemy was "thrown down." There is no evidence to suggest that God ever lost His omnipotent status; thus He is and was just as omnipotent as He always was. [Any discussions of large and small infinities, or degrees of uniqueness, are purposely avoided here.] Thus it must have been an issue of *authority.*

When God created the heavens and the earth, He had both the power and the authority. But after the enemy was thrown down, there is no other reasonable explanation other than God had the power, but had insufficient *authority* to completely stop the destruction. (It is not known what additional damage He may have prevented. This would be similar to calculating "jobs saved.")

And there is no other *reasonable* explanation, other than at some unspecified time later, He had insufficient authority to complete the redemption Himself—else why need and refer to *created* man as tsâbâ' (Hebrew), or "hosts?"

Thus the only *rational* conclusion, is that He had previously given some portion of His authority to something or someone else—and as we know; He was to do a similar thing; (granting the authority, but here also instructing said *created* hosts to put the "kibosh" on the earth); much later on.

Although admittedly this is a *derived* conclusion, it is the conclusion that makes the most sense, and best explains those things that are known. Some time after Genesis 1:1, God likely had introduced some type of life forms to the earth, and gave them control over the earth. Whether these represent the original *Atlanteans*, (from "Atlantis"), or some other beings is not known. Those beings who existed at that time, must have also had free will; but knew not; (as much later was to be the case with Adam); the dangers involved with the enemy. Having never encountered evil, they had no knowledge of good and evil; and thus represented "easy prey." The Bible; being a book about redemption and not a history book; (at least that portion which is agreed to by most or all as authentic; i.e.; the 66 Books); contains little direct historical information regarding many things, and thus derivation is necessary. Ergo; the subsequent instructions, (kibosh), to the *created* man or hosts, actually represented a *transfer* of the same authority God had initially relinquished and granted to those original, but now extinct, life forms.

If this somehow sounds a bit familiar; this is because "Eden" was actually the provision of an area similar to the condition of the earth before the enemy was "thrown down;" but with a similar but somewhat different purpose.

—*Some unspecified time about 6,000 - 8,000 years ago*

Genesis 2:8 tells us:

> "The LORD God planted a garden
> toward the east, in Eden;
> and there He placed the
> man whom He had formed."[9,7]

The fact that we are told that it was the "*formed*," man who was "*placed*," should not be overlooked.

> "Common belief is that Eden and
> the garden are synonymous; but verse
> 8 does not actually read that way. It
> reads that the garden was a section of
> Eden in the East, or at least toward the
> East. So then Eden; which is generally

believed to mean delight, or de-light, or "of or from" the light; was necessarily larger than the garden; this garden then being a subsection of Eden.

"The word garden is a bit misleading. The actual word for garden is "1588 gan from 1598; a *garden* (as *fenced*): - garden. 1598 ganan a prim. root; to *hedge* about, i.e. (gen.) *protect*: - defend" [9C]

"*Chambers* states that "garden" is "... related to *gart* enclosure, YARD; congnate with Old Saxon *gard*, Old English *geard*, Old Icelandic *gardhr*, Gothic *gard-s*, all with the meaning enclosure;..." [9D]

"The use of this term seems to have much more to do with security or protection, rather than simply a place to grow plants. A better definition would likely be a "guarded area;" the term "guarded," probably coming from the same (garden) root. But guarded in the sense of an enclosure, fence, hedged, protected etc, (not by a guard such as personnel), resulting in a *protected* area.

"The word "planted" is "5193 nata a prim. root; prop. to *strike* in, i.e. *fix*; spec. to *plant* (lit. or fig.): - fastened, plant (-er)."[9E]

"Planted or plants in the sense we use it as relating to horticulture; is a specific use of the broader meaning of the term "plant," relating to that specific (horticultural) purpose. In actuality, one does not in fact "plant a garden" when placing plants in a garden. The acts of selection of an area, preparing the soil, fencing in the area, etc., is the creation of the guarded area, garden or gan; these actions are entirely different and separate from placing the plants in said area.

"The use of "plant" in the general sense is to fix or fasten; as in "plant your feet firmly on the ground." The plantar surface of the foot being another related example. The word "supplant" or "supplanter," as in the meaning of Jacob's name, does in no way refer to a garden or gardening activities.

"So a better translation would be that God fixed or fastened a fence or hedge in East Eden, which resulted in a protective enclosure. And into that protected area, "He placed the man whom he had formed." It does not merely state that He placed *a* man. Nor does it state that He placed the man he had *created*. Neither of these can be true, because of the qualification by use of the term to describe this man. What He actually did place there, was the man He had "*formed.*"

"This does not really seem to make very much sense. Why would God create a protective area to place this formed man? What is it or was it that God could possibly need to protect this man from?"[9.8] [Excerpt from "*Meekraker Beginnings...*" Reprinted by Permission]

An extensive and detailed account of this time, can be found in "*MeekRaker Beginnings...*" But in short, the main purpose of the *formation* of Adam et seq.; was to begin the process of the redemption of the *immaterial* part of man, which is generally known as salvation or justification.

There was also to be substantial redemption of the *material* as well, but by a means other than by God alone. It is more than mere speculation to suggest that while existing in the *material* realm as a physically alive *man*; God "qualified," and thus was able to *legitimately* utilize the authority He had likely twice granted to others; but was unable to utilize, (*power* - but not the *authority*), from the *immaterial* realm.

Adam & Co. were formed *inside* the *gan*, or protected area; and remained there for some unspecified time. They were then banished, and thus were then *outside* of the gan. Had there been those who knew of this protected area, say any of the descendants of the originally created hosts; who then witnessed the exit of Adam & Co. from this area; (likely clothed in animal skins); said witnesses would likely have considered them as collectively being "one(s) from the other side," (from the *inside*), of this gan.

They would likely have called them whatever in their language meant: "one from the other side;" which of course is the actual definition of the word *Hebrew*. This is also why so much of the Hebrew language is derived from Chaldean.

The *true* Chaldeans; such as the ancestors of those already in the city of Ur at the time of Abraham's birth—those who existed long before the formation of Adam; likely spoke Chaldean, and thus Chaldean was likely the language Adam & Co.; i.e.; the very *first* Hebrews; learned after exiting, (going out to the other side of), the gan.

Thus although today *gentile*, is considered as meaning "non-Jewish," this was not always so; and in fact still is not so—any such usage notwithstanding. *Gentile* refers to the *created* hosts and their descendants. *Hebrew* refers to those that were *formed*, and came "from the other side" of the gan, and their descendants.

Where does this leave man today?

As a matter of degree, mankind has evolved in many ways and overall has made many positive changes with regard to the redemption of the earth. As a binary, the situation; particularly man's situation; remains unchanged. Meaning: The earth is not yet completely redeemed, (unredeemed); and will remain so until events described in

Revelation come to pass. Who decides when this will be? Man of course, depending on how his free will is exercised.

Man therefore remains with those aforementioned instructions contained in Genesis 1:28, as *material* redemption remains an act *in progress*.

> *"multiply, and replenish the earth,*
> *and subdue it: and have*
> *dominion over the fish of the sea,*
> *and over the fowl of the air, and*
> *over every living thing that*
> *moveth upon the earth."*

And thus man has free will with regard to decisions; but has little or no free will with respect to any and all consequences, (karma), of these actions. How does one obtain consequences or karma to his liking? The answer; is to act in a manner which will produce consequences or karma to his liking. This requires clear, and long term thinking. In the absence of sufficient information, *morality* based action, is the best, (and usually the most difficult), action.

The *logically derived* beings that likely existed between Genesis 1:1 and Genesis 1:2, initially also had no knowledge of, (or experience with), *evil*. When the source of all evil was "thrown down;" they knew not with what they were "dealing." The result was total extermination of themselves, and every other "*form*" on the earth; leaving the earth with respect to its original condition, essentially "*void.*"

There is not much reliable Biblical information available regarding those *created* hosts, who were instructed to "put the kibosh" on the earth; and the common conflation of *created* and *formed* causes confusion. It seems logical however; that they would have understood that there was another entity involved; i.e.; that which must be fought and defeated, in order to fulfill these instructions.

When Adam & Co. were *formed*, there was no evil in *their* environment—the same being the very purpose of the gan or protected area—irrespective of *their* lack of any knowledge regarding so much as even the possibility of the existence of evil. It was only after the enemy was *introduced* to the area; that their actions resulted not in the continuation of harmony, but rather ultimately resulted in their banishment to the "other side."

In the absolute or binary sense, in terms of *process*; nothing has changed since that time; and man has free will as a "God given" right—irrespective of any and all attempts by man to negate this. Man has the right to make free will decisions, and is held responsible for those decisions by the "law of compensation;" known as karma by some, and $F=MA$ with equal and opposite reactions by others.

If it is stipulated that "good" or "upright" here means consistent with God's will; and "evil" means against God's will; then any action which "moves the ball" *toward redemption* of the earth is "good."

Similarly; any action or actions that *interferes* with the *redemption* of the earth, is "evil."

The most fundamental requirement in this process of material redemption is man's free will. Without free will; (i.e.; with manipulation); there would be little or no difference between man; who has been given some degree of exclusive authority engaging in these actions; and God Himself engaging in these actions, but *ultra-vires*.

Either case would be an unbalanced and thus *unjust* act. Irrespective of anything else, it is clear that God gave the authority over the earth to the created hosts; i.e.; man, in Genesis 1:28. God cannot simultaneously allocate authority over anything, and at the same time maintain said authority Himself. Hence the utilization of this very same authority by God, would then necessarily usurp the previously granted authority, making said authority "situationally dependent."

Therefore; it seems the most fundamental or "baseline" evil act, is any attempt to abridge the free will of man; unless said free will interferes with the expression of the rights of another. The only other exception, is or would be through obtaining man's free will decision to permit any such interference *before the fact*. This forms the basis of *just* government.

God's primary means of causing man to make upright decisions; is education, (truth, or that which *is*); and the *primary* source; but by no means the *sole* source of this education is the Bible. But in order to obtain this information, one must be capable of understanding what it actually teaches.

The enemy knows this, which is why there are not only translations; but *versions* of the Bible. Here the enemy is hoping to be not only the *first*, but the *only* to plead the case, *without* another examining it. (See Proverbs 18:17)

The enemy's *primary* means of causing man to make evil decisions is *manipulation*. This is done most especially by thoughts, ideas, and suggestions; as essentially explained by Peter; and by providing misinformation; (lies, or *that which is not*); via many means, unfortunately including portions of the many "versions" of the Bible.

In order to establish what constitutes "good" and "evil;" in the *governmental* sense; i.e. governmental *actions*; again with "good" here meaning in furtherance of God's will; and "evil" meaning against God's will; some type of tests for actions should be established. This is as opposed to say "wicked," as referring to the *nature* of the act itself. Here in the *governmental* sense; "good" and "evil" refer to *any* governmental act's consistency with God's will. By these definitions, what happened at Calvary was both "good" and "wicked."

The first and most basic test should be whether or not the expression of *free will* is being abridged; and if so, is this being done *justly*. As previously stated, any interference with the expression of free will must pass one of two tests. In order to be *just*, there must be either reasonable and clear and present likelihood of interference with *another's* rights; or there must be consent to this interference by the governed *before the fact*.

Whether or not second hand smoke is dangerous in any significant way, currently remains unknown—the magnitude of the quantity of folderol claiming the contrary notwithstanding.

Whether or not what is now called "climate change," is in any significant way the result of man's actions, also remains currently unknown. Perhaps both are true, both are false or perhaps there is some racemic mixture of truth. To state that either has been proven by statistics or science; requires either that one redefine statistics, science, and evidence; or utilize different terms such as "docudrama."

Yet the expression of free will of millions of citizens is being interfered with by purporting "clear and present" dangers, where no evidence exists for the same. One is the interference of the free will of an establishment owner to *permit* a legal behavior, and/or the free will of the patron to *engage* in said otherwise legal behavior. The other is the expropriation of billions of dollars of wealth from citizens under false pretenses—if science and evidence are the criteria. Thus these represent nothing more than manipulation by purporting that that which is in fact *not*, as that which in fact *is*.

As is generally the case with liberals vs. statists, the difference here, is that true *liberals* believe that such evidence exists; while *statists* either know full well that it does not, or simply do not care. It is the public health interests and environmental interests that motivate true liberals; while the statists are solely interested in the *control* and the *money*; i.e.; the *power*. And primarily the power or *control*, because free will is foundational for all that follows. In addition; power or control ultimately begats wealth, in proportion to the amount of power or control.

In a broader sense, if it is so stipulated that the instructions to the individual "hosts," as contained in Genesis 1:28 to: "*multiply, and replenish the earth, and subdue it: and have dominion over the fish of the sea, and over the fowl of the air, and over every living thing that moveth upon the earth*;" are God's instructions regarding the function of man; then how do the statist's positions "score" on the "evil scale?"

It seems in almost, if not all cases; the statist's positions are *contrary* to the instructions contained in Genesis 1:28, and thus are *evil* by definition.

Even if the previously discussed unique role and purpose of man in the *redemption* of the earth could somehow be ignored; it nevertheless remains clear that it is God's will for man to substantially alter the condition of the earth towards *greater* not *lesser* levels of organization, from what it was at the time man was given these instructions.

There are reasons why statists are so radically *pro-abortion*—any mendacious claims of "choice" notwithstanding. This represents a manifestation of their disdain of the first part of these instructions; (*multiply* and replenish the earth)— whether they are aware of these instructions or not.

On this point, the enemy agrees with them completely, and for understandable, (but not "good"), reason(s). The enemy knows that decreasing the numbers of *his* enemies makes victories for him more likely. He simply, (and quite correctly), believes that having to fight fewer battles, because of fewer "hosts," makes winning the war more likely.

The concept that "free will" represents either "a," or "the," foundational requirement, in order for man to carry out his role according to God's instructions; *presupposes* the presence of physical life. Without the presence of physical life, man cannot exercise free will from this, (the material), realm.

For the enemy; the avoidance of this necessary prerequisite of life solves many potential problems for him that might otherwise manifest. For the "pre-existing" statists; human life represents a condition to the statists which has a bit of "schizophrenic" reality.

The statist's view; is that there must be many human beings to control, and from whom wealth can be seized. But at the same time; there is at best no respect for human life, and arguably *contempt* for human life. The answer to this paradox of course forms a basis for eugenics.

Again, it is ironic that statists utilize the concept of "choice" in furtherance of these objectives. This is done in order to avoid certain types of liabilities. Although statists believe that they are somehow immune to the constraints and effects of natural law; they also realize that at least in the US, they generally are not yet immune to the effects of man's laws—despite the fact that they believe that they should be. At least for the present, statists simply cannot force the termination of human life, without the risks of serious consequences to them. Other countries have at times devised schemes whereby forced abortion is legal, but the US has not yet degraded to this point.

So statists rely on what they consider to be the "choice" paradigm. It is then not the statists who are *directly* aborting, or directly causing the aborting, of an embryo or a fetus; but rather it is the "mother's" *choice*.

This is precisely why statists object to too much information being provided to the "mother." Statists prefer that the *only* information provided, would be that which would result in abortion being the only reasonable course of action. Physical evidence such as sonograms, and discussion of alternatives such as adoption; might lead the "mother" to believe that there are reasonable alternatives to abortion, and thus in the statist's view should never be presented.

This of course in no way represents "informed consent," as true informed consent requires that *all* reasonable alternatives be presented prior to making a choice. Rather, this represents classic *manipulation*; here by willful omission of pertinent information. Thus the *reality* of the situation to the "mother," by statist intention; precludes the inclusion of any *realities* from any *actualities* that may result in a different decision. Thus this clearly also fails the "free will" test.

Statists object to energy being used to make positive changes in virtually all of its forms. Fossil fuels pollute the earth, so both their acquisition and usage must be prohibited. Nuclear energy is too "dangerous," despite its factual history. Even solar power scars the landscape, and wind turbines kill birds. Conservation is surely a good thing, as long as the motives are to increase efficiency and decrease pollution. But statists primary motive is to limit man's activity, (and thus limit compliance with Genesis 1:28); with only a secondary concern for the environment, if at all. Thus this also fails the "free will" test.

Statists would rather see human beings subjected to starvation and bankruptcy in order to protect some obscure life form; than to provide an alternative means of protecting said life form. There is no balance of interests, but rather only absolutes. On its face, this often seems absurd, but that is because the true purposes remain hidden. Thus this also fails the "free will" test.

In order to "kibosh" the earth as instructed in Genesis 1:28; this requires *people*, and *means* for changes. This is similar to the age-old motive, opportunity, and means requirements for the commission of a crime; but here the "crime" is carrying out said instructions. And it seems that statists do in fact believe, that this, in and of itself, either is, or should be punishable as a crime— irrespective of any *nocere*, or harm, to any living or non-living entity.

And so it seems that there are two separate and distinct conditions of the earth:

The first being that condition in which the earth was in at the end of Genesis 1:1; and partially described at or near the end of the Book of Revelation. This was, and will be the earth as designed, requiring no "kiboshing;" i.e.; balanced and harmonious.

Then there is the second; or the earth as described in Genesis 1:2 and onward. This represents an imperfect earth, requiring perfecting.

God began this perfecting or redeeming as described in the verses that follow, doing what he could do without usurping previously transferred authority. God then created man to continue this process, and instructed man to do so.

Thus what is ubiquitously considered as "normal," is actually the "exception." Meaning; that the current condition of the earth and the life forms upon it, are not that which exist by design; but rather represent a *transitional* state, and thus the exception.

The true "normal;" is that condition which was described at the conclusion of Genesis 1:1. And it is the purpose of man as hosts or tsâbâ', to continue this process until its completion as described partially in Revelation.

It is also clear that there were and are two forces involved:

That which is described at the *end* of Genesis 1:1, represents the results of one force. That which was described at the *beginning* of Genesis 1:2, represents the results of another force, acting upon that which was described at the end of Genesis 1:1.

Neither situation has changed in the binary or absolute sense; although there has been considerable improvement; i.e.; *perfecting* of the earth. There have been "peaks and valleys" in this effort, but the overall trend has been towards restoration. And there have been those who have attempted to "reshape" the earth according to *their* desires; e.g.; Hitler, Stalin, Mao, etc; and present day statists.

There is also the matter of the present day "Radical Islamic Terrorists;" and their perverse view of that which essentially represents a form of Abrahamic quasi-Judaism—but here Judaism not according to *Abraham*, but according to *Ishmael*.

The very literal meaning of Islam, roughly meaning *to submit*; refers to submission to *God's* will, and not the will of man. Any such radical "movements," (euphemism), that do not respect free will and human life cannot be of God. Or perhaps stated better; to the extent that any group does not respect free will and human life, then to that very same extent cannot be of God.

Each of these forces is continuing to act in order to restore one of these two conditions. God is and has been utilizing man as tsâbâ' in furtherance of the restoration of the conditions as described at the end of Genesis 1:1; and the enemy has also been utilizing man, but in furtherance of the "restoration" of the conditions as described at the beginning of Genesis 1:2.

Man, with *free will*, remains in the middle. "Free will" makes it *just* for man to choose to act in accordance with God's will. As previously stated, without free will, there would essentially be no difference in man acting, and God Himself acting, but acting *ultra-vires*; and thus unjustly.

193

One might reasonably ask, for what possible reason(s) would an omnipotent God create man, and then assign man to this job; rather than just "finishing the job" Himself? By Hobson's choice, as previously discussed, the answer must of course be the authority.

Man is under constant attack by the enemy, including lies and the perversion of the truth. It is the individual man that must decide what it is he *will*, or *will* not do; and precisely what he *will*, or *will* not, "put up" with. Robert Heinlein once stated, (paraphrased): "You cannot enslave a free man. The most you can do is kill him."

History has its own "trash bin," and the same is replete with those who had the same idea as the statists; long before any of the grandfathers of present day statists were even contemplated, much less born.

The use of the word "progressive" with respect to politics, is particularly heinous. In other usages, *progressive* has a positive connotation; as after all who would want to be "regressive, or "stuck standing still?"

But *politically*, "progressive" has nothing to do with improvement; i.e.; *progress*; but rather it simply means to break injustices into small units, in order allow sufficient time for acceptance or "socialization." Most frogs will in fact jump out, if placed in that pot of boiling water. Those that are placed in cold water that is slowly heated to boiling, generally will remain, because the changes are gradual. Although present day statists did not invent this, they know and utilize this technique quite well.

A "life of crime," begins the very same way. "It's only a quarter," being proffered with respect to a theft being acceptable, changes the *binary* of not stealing, to a *relative* matter depending upon the *amount* or *value* of the theft.

The commandment against stealing, presents no such threshold or distinction. This *amount* is then easily modified depending upon exigencies of life, until one is caught—and generally not even knowing how they got to that level of theft.

This is precisely why "any and all" unjust governmental actions must be opposed at the outset. If one becomes the target of invective because of this; the same should be considered as mere diversion, and admission of the lack of facts in support of the unjust actions.

One only need look at the Δ or differences between presidential candidates in the not so distant past. By today's standards, both candidates in 1960 would be considered as conservative, with relatively minor differences—JFK, (the democrat), having cut taxes and boosted the military.

The 2016 presidential election featured perhaps the most stark political differences in recent political memory. One candidate favored open borders and amnesty, tax increases, and abortion on demand, including "partial birth abortion." The other candidate proffered building a physical wall with the deportation of all illegal aliens, law and order, tax cuts, and was, (and still is), pro-life.

Brit Hume correctly stated that Barack Obama's *legacy*, was in fact the election of Donald Trump. This represented the "reset" of a government steadily moving to the left for many decades. [The Biblical mechanism of the "Trump win," is non-politically explained in detail in: "*Donald Trump Candidacy According to Matthew?*"]

As hosts or tsâbâ'; H. Sapiens as per instructions, are required to determine which *policies*; and thus which *candidates*, are in furtherance of said instructions. Any policy or candidate proffering *any* infringement of the expression of free will that does not meet the aforementioned exceptions, should be immediately disavowed—irrespective of how many it would be that they would "save" being proffered

It is not news that government is a "necessary evil." But when said necessary evil produces more evil than it remediates, it is the *responsibility* of man to make the necessary and appropriate changes.

And in their wisdom, the founding fathers provided the lawful means by which this is to be done.

Chapter 10

The Pseudo-Statists

Thus far, those who are involved with and utilize "the state" for control have been discussed. Once again, these believe: "*the state is therefore not subject to God the Bible natural law, or any other religion or ethical system.*"

But given the 24/7 attacks of the enemy, what about others? Specifically; those who *do not* believe that they are *not*: "*not subject to God the Bible natural law, or any other religion or ethical system;*" i.e.; those that readily admit that they *are* in fact subject to "*God the Bible natural law, or any other religion or ethical system?*" Is it possible that these are somehow 100% successful against said 24/7 attacks 100% of the time?

No effort is being made here to attribute anything to religions(s) in the general sense. In addition; what is being utilized is not what *others* might state about religion in general; or about any specific denomination. Rather; what is being utilized here, is what it is that said religious denomination(s) *themselves*, are in fact stating about themselves—via official pronouncements, or their recognized "authorities."

Once again re-examining a portion of that which David Brin is attributed with having stated, might be illuminating: "*It is said that power corrupts, but actually it's more true that power attracts the corruptible. The sane are usually attracted by other things than power.*"

Again, Brin is speaking of power here in the *general* sense. Although this is usually considered to relate to *governmental* power, which is one type or a subset of "power;" it is *power* itself in the broader sense to which he is referring.

Ephesians 2:8-9 (KJV) tells us:

> *"For by grace are ye saved through faith;*
> *and that not of yourselves:*
> *it is the gift of God:*
> *Not of works, lest any man should boast."*[10.1]

Strictly from the standpoint of *analysis*, it matters little whether one is a "Christian" or not. One not need be a Christian, in order to understand what it is that "Christians" believe. *Knowing* what it is that Christianity actually states; is entirely different than *believing* that that which Christianity states, is in fact true.

The actual Greek word translated here in Ephesians as "grace" is:

> "*5485* charis; from *5463*; *graciousness* (as *gratifying*), of manner or act..."[10.2]

A fair definition of *grace*, is *receiving* something of positive value that is *not* deserved. This is in contrast to *mercy*; which is *not receiving* something of negative value that *is* deserved.

Here we are told by Paul that we are saved by "*grace*," and that this is accomplished "*through faith*."

This sounds suspiciously more like payment, rather than any type of grace. Meaning; *if* you believe, *then* your payment is salvation.

Here it at first appears that the "*works*," is the faith that creates the imbalance; and the balance for this "work" is the granting of salvation. This of course would not be grace, and most certainly would then not qualify as any type of "*gift*." Rather; salvation would clearly be the result of "*works*"—notwithstanding that any possibility of this cause-effect relationship existing, is clearly negated at the end of the citation.

The key word here is: "*through*."

Here the actual Greek word translated as "through" is:

> "*1223* dia; a prim. prep. denoting a *channel* of an act; *through* (in very wide applications..."[10.3]

Thus the *balancing* of an existing imbalance by obtaining salvation; is *not* the result of any imbalance that may be *caused* by faith. Faith merely provides the *channel* by which salvation is obtained. The imbalance already exists and has existed since Calvary. Faith merely provides a *channel* for salvation; and in no way contributes to any pre-existing imbalance caused by faith, which is then resolved or balanced by the granting of salvation.

When a channel is provided in a dam for water to escape, there are no pumps involved. There is no energy involved other than that required for the provision of the channel. The imbalance already exists, and the water will flow once the channel is provided. We are likewise told by Paul that salvation; like this water, will flow once there is a channel; and that faith provides that channel. Here faith in and of itself does not in any way "pay for" or create any *imbalance*, which salvation then balances—as the imbalance already exists. This is why salvation is both grace and a gift as it is "*not of yourselves: it is the gift of God.*"

It is true that faith can create many imbalances in many areas, which can then be balanced many different positive ways. But salvation is not one of these.

Similarly; we are told that salvation is: "*Not of works, lest any man should boast.*"

The original Greek word translated as "works" is:

"2041 ĕrgŏn; from a prim. (but obsol.) ĕrgō (to *work*); to *toil* (as an effort or occupation) by impl. an act."[10.4]

Erg is the root of the word ergonomics. An "erg" is a unit used for the measurement of energy.

Thus we are told that there is no imbalance caused or possible by works or ĕrgŏn, whose balancing mechanism could possibly be salvation. Just as is the case with faith; works can also create many imbalances in many areas, which can then be balanced many different ways. But again, salvation is not one of these.

"It ain't bragging if you can do it."[10.5]—Dizzy Dean

This is quite true. It is not bragging if you can do it—but it *is boasting* if you can do it. A *boast* represents that which *is*; while *bragging*; (braggadocio); represents that which *is not*.

The actual Greek word translated in Ephesians 2:9 as "boast" is:

"2744 kauchaŏmai; from some (obsol.) base akin to that of auchĕō (to *boast*) and 2172; to *vaunt* (in a good or bad sense)..."[10.6]

Thus when Paul tells us: "*Not of works, lest any man should boast;*" this confirms the falsity of any "*works*" related cause for salvation. "*Any man*" can surely *brag* about salvation being the result of his works; but of course this represents falsehood—

because Paul tells us that he ("*any man*") can't actually *boast* about it, because he "cannot do it;" as salvation is unrelated to works.

Ephesians 2:4 tells us:

> *"But God, who is rich in mercy,*
> *for his great love wherewith he loved us,"*[10.7]

The actual Greek word translated as "mercy" is:

> "1656   ĕlĕŏs; of uncert. affin.; compassion (human or divine espec. active)"[10.8]

Titus 3:5 tells us:

> *"Not by works of righteousness*
> *which we have done,*
> *but according to his mercy he saved us,*
> *by the washing of regeneration,*
> *and renewing of the Holy Ghost;"*[10.9]

Here in Titus, Paul is reaffirming that not by any works; even works of *righteousness*; are we saved, but "according to his *mercy*."

The introduction of *mercy* here in Titus is also:

"*1656* ĕlĕŏs; of uncert. affin.; *compassion* (human or divine espec. active)."[10.10]

Earlier in Ephesians, it was *charis*, translated as "grace;" which was a causative factor. Here in Titus, the same is so for mercy. Thus salvation is described as both *grace*; i.e.; receiving something of positive value, (salvation), that is *not* deserved; and also *mercy*; i.e.; *not* receiving something of negative value, (eternal separation from God), that *is* or would otherwise be deserved.

———————

What is a "mortal sin?"
According to Colin B. Donovan, STL, from *etwn.com*:

> "Mortal sin is called mortal because it is the 'spiritual' death of the soul (separation from God). If we are in the state of grace it loses this supernatural life for us. If we die without repenting we will lose Him for eternity."[10.11]

Here Donovan seems to be stating that mortal sin will alter the "state of grace;" i.e.; salvation by justification; to that very same state which existed prior to obtaining said "state of grace."
This seems to be a *variant* of the common definition of *justification*. Justification is often

considered to mean: "just as though one never sinned." Here Donovan seems to make a similar argument with respect to the commission of a mortal sin. According to Donovan, it seems that the commission of a mortal sin is: "just as though one never received salvation."

Thus by only minor extension, although *works* cannot in any way *provide* salvation; it seems that according to Donovan, certain *works* can *remove* salvation, or this "state of grace."

However Paul just told us that it is *faith* and not works which provides the *channel* for salvation; and that salvation is unrelated to works. Given this *channel* provided by faith, salvation will flow of its own accord, without any additional action. Since it is faith alone that opens this channel and not works; it must be asked as to the mechanism whereby this channel can be *blocked* by works. The answer is that it cannot, as no relationship exists between works, and the establishment of this channel for salvation/justification.

However; Donovan provides an "out" for the commission of mortal sin—*repenting*.

According to Donovan, "repenting" is:

> "receiving the Sacrament of Penance
> we are restored to His friendship.
> Catholics are not allowed to receive
> Communion if they have unconfessed
> mortal sins."[10.12]

The root or the "pent" part of *repent* is the "Latin *penitire*, to regret."[10.13]

But the word is not "pent" but rather *repent*. This could reasonably be defined as not *to regret*, but rather to *regret again*. The word repentance does not generally mean to receive any type of Sacrament; and neither does it generally mean to make any type of formal confession to any third party.

According to "*aboutcatholics.com:*"

> "'Mortal' means death; they are sins that cause death to the soul. Mortal sins completely sever one's relationship with God and the sacrament of Penance and Reconciliation (commonly called Confession) is necessary to restore this relationship."[10.14]

So it seems that although according to Paul, salvation cannot be obtained by any type of works; righteous or otherwise; according to others, it somehow can nevertheless be *removed* by works; if and when said works constitute a *mortal* sin.

If merely for the purposes of discussion, this is stipulated to be true; it must be asked as to what the change in status is? Meaning; what is the difference between one who is unsaved; and one who is or "was" saved, but then his "works" were such that a commission of a mortal sin occurred?

Paul tells us that salvation has nothing to do with works, but only faith. There is no cause-effect relationship between works and salvation. Rather; it is *faith* that opens this *dia* or channel, whereby salvation is then delivered. Like merely opening the front door, and there is an automatic pizza delivery at no cost—because a lifetime of pizza has already been paid for. All that is required is an opening for delivery.

Paul tells us that salvation does not represent any type of payment or "karma;" but rather is a gift of grace or mercy or "compassion"—depending upon one's perspective. The availability of salvation is like potential energy, which requires only a *dia* or channel; here the channel provided by faith, and faith alone.

So if one is unsaved, all that is required is this dia or channel; which is created by faith, and faith alone; and whose existence is completely unrelated to any works. This is Paul's position.

But others claim, that although this, (Paul's position), may be true; works that fit into the "mortal sin" category, can remove this salvation. And according to this same theory, maintaining this *dia* or channel with faith, is now insufficient to maintain or restore said saved status. Presumably, mortal sin now blocks this dia or channel, and despite the fact that faith alone originally provided this dia or channel, said blockage cannot be removed by faith alone—unlike the "original" blockage. Instead: "Penance and Reconciliation (commonly called Confession)" is necessary to "reopen" this channel, or "restore this relationship."

What is "commonly called confession," consists of the *works* of seeking out and "confessing" one's sins to a third party, and thus not directly to God.

Said third party then advises as to what the penance for this mortal and other sin commission is to be—and these (penance) *works*, usually consist of some level of repetitive prayer. Once these *works* are all completed, the presumed blockage is removed, the "petitioner" is "good to go" in the salvation department—at least until next time.

It remains unclear as to the logic behind the theory regarding precisely how it is that although faith alone, and not any works, is sufficient to *provide* this *dia* or channel; but nevertheless works are required in order to maintain or *restore* this channel.

It also remains unclear as to how it is; that although God provides salvation the first time; any future provision of salvation, (assuming it actually can be lost by works), cannot be provided by God alone; but rather now requires a man to assist Him.

It is likewise unclear as to why it is that *initial* gift of salvation is completely unrelated to works; but any "*subsequent*" provision of salvation requires works, and thus must be "paid for."

This theory also seems patently unfair. According to *Paul*, even those such as Hitler, Stalin, Tojo, and others; even if locked in a bunker alone; were *alone* capable of receiving salvation in the last seconds of their life, simply by faith.

But according to *others*, one who had already received salvation by faith, and was also alone and locked in the same or a similar bunker; would be in big trouble, had they committed any sin characterized as mortal *after* being saved. In the absence of any third party, how could these purported required works take place?

Donovan goes on to cite 1 Cor. 6:9-10 in support of this.[10.15]

1 Cor. 6:9-10 (KJV) tells us:

> "*Know ye not that the unrighteous*
> *shall not inherit the kingdom of God?*
> *Be not deceived: neither fornicators,*
> *nor idolaters, nor adulterers,*
> *nor effeminate, nor abusers*
> *of themselves with mankind,*
>
> *Nor thieves, nor covetous,*
> *nor drunkards, nor revilers,*
> *nor extortioners,*
> *shall inherit the kingdom of God.*"[10.16]

These above verses cited by Donovan, sound quite supportive of Donovan's position—unless and until the very next verse, (1 Cor. 6:11) is read.

1 Cor. 6:11 (KJV) tells us:

> "*And such were some of you:*
> *but ye are washed,*
> *but ye are sanctified,*
> *but ye are justified in the name*
> *of the Lord Jesus,*
> *and by the Spirit of our God.*"[10.17]

According to Fox News in March of 2008:

> "After 1,500 years the Vatican has
> brought the seven deadly sins up to
> date by adding seven new ones for the
> age of globalization... The new deadly
> sins include polluting, genetic
> engineering, being obscenely rich,
> drug dealing, abortion, pedophilia and
> causing social injustice."[10.18]

The two most interesting new "mortal" sins seem
to be: "being obscenely rich," and "causing social
injustice;" as these, unlike sins such as murder or
adultery; are not binaries.

It is unclear as to the difference between "being
rich" and "being obscenely rich." Likewise it is
unclear as to *who* it is that makes this
determination, or precisely *how* this determination
is made.

The threshold for the aforementioned mortal
sins murder and adultery are clear. Without some
type of corpse, there can be no murder. And with
respect to adultery as commonly understood, there
has to be—well there either is or is not binary
evidence. But being "obscenely rich," as opposed
to just "rich," is not a binary, but rather is an
"analog," as well as a *subjective* determination.

In the absence of clear and objective standards,
adjusted for inflation of course; the average person
simply cannot determine if or when they cross the
threshold from merely "being rich," to "being
obscenely rich."

It should be noted that with respect to the *love* of money, 1 Timothy 6:10 (KJV) tells us:

> *"For the love of money is the root of all evil:*
> *which while some coveted after,*
> *they have erred from the faith,*
> *and pierced themselves*
> *through with many sorrows."*[10.19]

But it should also be noted that with respect to the *very money itself,* Ecclesiastes 10:19 (KJV) tells us:

> *"A feast is made for laughter,*
> *and wine maketh merry:*
> *but money answereth all things."*[10.20]

Thus this mortal sin of "being obscenely rich," (having an obscenely large amount of money); means that someone committing this new mortal sin; simultaneously and necessarily then also has an "obscenely" large amount of answers—at least according to Ecclesiastes.

It is also unclear as to the remedy for: "being obscenely rich." This is not a singular event that has a definable ending, such as murder or adultery as commonly understood. With these, one can "repent" in both the literal and "Sacramental" sense, to a *fait accompli*.

But being "rich;" irrespective of the level of obscenity; is an ongoing issue. If one gives his wealth away for good reason, this would result in only a temporary diminution of the level of wealth to that which is considered below the "obscene" level. Once karma, or F = MA and equal and opposite reactions occur; the level of wealth will once again pierce this "obscene" threshold, resulting in an even higher degree of "obscenity;"— perhaps an even greater "mortal sin." It seems that the only true way to avoid continual commission of this mortal sin; would be to give away some portion of the wealth for reasons that are not good, thereby incurring negative karma or loss.

It also must be asked how this new mortal sin comports with Deuteronomy 28:2?

Deuteronomy 28:2 (KJV) tells us:

> "*And all these blessings shall
> come on thee,
> and overtake thee,
> if thou shalt hearken unto the
> voice of the LORD thy God.*"[10,21]

It seems that hearkening "*unto the voice of the Lord thy God,*" could easily result in blessings which will result in a level of wealth well beyond the "obscene" level.

Here God would have to be careful as to make certain that the level which will "overtake thee," consistently remains below the *man determined* "obscene" level—else it would be God Himself who would become an "accessory before the fact," to the commission, and continued commission of this new "mortal sin."

The new mortal sin of "causing social injustice;" is even more difficult to understand. It seems that the "woe to(s)" contained in Isaiah and elsewhere, "cover" those who are in power—irrespective of the seemingly consistent ignoring of this admonition by the same.

But here it seems that this "causing social injustice" mortal sin, is not limited to those who violate their fiduciary responsibilities to those who trusted them, and willfully granted them the same. Rather; it seems that this sin can be committed by anyone at any time.

Is it "causing social injustice;" to get the best price possible on a new car? After all, there are ramifications to the seller for the buyer willfully paying the seller less than one can. Is it "causing social injustice;" to drive a vehicle that others cannot afford? Is it "causing social injustice;" to not feed the hungry?

After all, Matthew 25:40 (KJV) tells us:

> *"Verily I say unto you, Inasmuch as ye
> have done it unto one of the least of
> these my brethren,
> ye have done it unto me."*[10.22]

But the person who does not *feed* the hungry, did not *cause* them to *become* hungry. Assuming that hunger falls into the "social injustice" category, the causative factor lies outside of the person who encountered the hungry person.

Rather it is the failure to provide a *remedy* to the pre-existing seeming injustice of hunger, to which this passage refers. Can it be stated that *failing* to *remedy* "social injustice" is the same as "causing social injustice?" And how can it be determined that the state of hunger is in itself a "social injustice?"

It must also be remembered that 2 Thessalonians 3:10-12 tells us:

> *"For even when we were with you,*
> *this we commanded you,*
> *that if any would not work,*
> *neither should he eat.*
>
> *For we hear that there are some*
> *which walk among you disorderly,*
> *working not at all, but are busybodies.*
>
> *Now them that are such we command*
> *and exhort by our Lord Jesus Christ,*
> *that with quietness they work,*
> *and eat their own bread."*[10.23]

Here in these passages, it seems that the referenced state of hunger is not any type of social *injustice*, but rather *justice*—at least according to Paul. Choosing to be one of the "busybodies," instead of working, is choosing non-productivity.

Is it social justice to consume the efforts of others because of this choice—assuming it is a choice? Meaning; that one is capable of some level of productivity, but chooses not to; and instead, relies upon consuming the fruits of the labors of others in order to survive. How is this justice to the worker?

It seems that that "causing social injustice," can be pretty much what anyone determines it to be. And this is especially serious here, in that it is a "mortal sin" that is the penalty. How could a "lay person," reliably decide what constitutes violations of such a serious nature? One best then rely upon and trust others as experts to decide what constitutes this sin, and then behave accordingly. Does this sound a bit familiar?

While conducting research for this tome, interviews were conducted with one who was taught Catholicism by Dominican nuns many years ago. This person; (hereafter "he"); recounted other behaviors taught as "mortal sins" at that time. One was failure to attend church on Sunday, or any other "Holy Day of Obligation." Eating meat on Fridays was another, although this was later changed.

He was also taught that receiving Holy Communion on nine consecutive "First Fridays," would guarantee that he could not die without a priest at his side. As a child he did in fact do this;

and then made a lifelong commitment to *stay away from priests*.

No efforts are being made here to in any way disparage any religion or religious beliefs. To the contrary, religions have been instrumental in disseminating the knowledge about the availability of salvation—irrespective of any deviations from what was originally taught.

But although the *ends* of religion and statism may *sometimes* be entirely different, there seem to be striking resemblances in the *means*—if it can be stipulated that each is primarily concerned with a different realm.

The statists are concerned with that which is in the material realm. More likely than not, they do not in any way seriously believe in any type of existence in any other realm. They promulgate very serious penalties *here* and *now,* if one does not behave in a manner to *their* liking. The use of "*their*" here is in contradistinction to "just" laws, where there "their liking" means with the agreement of the citizenry.

The "religious folk" are concerned with not merely the material realm, but also eternal existence in another, (the immaterial), realm. They promulgate penalties in this *immaterial* realm, if one does not behave on a manner to *their* liking in this material realm. But here "their" liking is supposed to be based upon a higher authority; i.e.; to *God's* liking, as per His written word. And some of this is in fact quite commendable. Proffering obedience to The Commandments, (of which there are not ten), represents good instruction.

However even God Himself; at least in Exodus 20; did not require *obedience*, but rather only that we *shâmar*; or *keep* these Commandments. As previously discussed, "Keep" or *shâmar* does not mean obey, but rather to guard them as though surrounded by a hedge of thorns. One "keeps" one's car in a garage for protection.

Men are asked to *keep* these Commandments at the ready when "decision making time" arrives; and incorporate these as instructions into this same decision making process.

God did not engage in interference of man's free will even to the extent of requiring *obedience* to His Commandments—at least at the time He announced them. There is that mess afterwards with "Hebrew slaves" and such; but the authenticity of this is highly suspect. Man is free to obey or disobey His Commandments, and will receive a return in accordance with his choices.

But religions often do that which even God himself would not do. Religions often attempt to not *influence* behavior by the provision of knowledge; but rather *coerce* behavior by promulgating severe penalties in the thereafter, for failure to engage in the type of "works" religions prefer in the "here and now."

This is *compulsion* at best, *manipulation* at worst; and although the *ends* of upright behavior are commendable, these *means* are not of God. Religions often create "clear and present dangers" to salvation, when no such danger can reasonably even be *derived* from His Word.

Sometimes this is done with best of intentions, and sometimes not. There are those who truly care so much, that these types of judgmental errors occur. But it must be asked that if these intentions were used as pavement; where would the road lead? Intentions alone were insufficient to prevent higher incidences of illegal drug use by those who completed the "program."

And of course there are those who are merely utilizing *religion* instead of *politics*, for statist type control. And of these, some in fact actually utilize both.

Most believe that "judgment day" is where or when that immaterial part of man is to be judged. A more compelling argument is that "judgment day," is not when a man is judged; but rather where or when man *receives* his judgment—with the actual judging having occurred prior to this. This judgment is a binary. Either that immaterial part is to be reunited with it source, or it is not.

It cannot be overemphasized that although one can simply walk away from any *religion* that doesn't make sense, and find one that does; *government* is a bit different. Any and all changes must be made within the governmental system previously agreed upon; unless and until said system is *justly* changed.

There is a "social contract theory," under which men govern themselves. This must be adhered to when changes are being made. Any proponents of "revolution" outside of these constraints; would be guilty of proffering as much or perhaps even more *unjust* actions than even those of the statists.

Chapter 11

The Phantom Verse

Chapter 11 is intentionally left blank, *in memory* of Matthew 17:21.

Chapter 12

Afterword

Wwhen one suddenly receives that one tiny piece of information, and it all "just comes together," the result is often: "Ahhh... Now I understand."

Faced with otherwise seemingly inconsistent facts, nothing makes any sense until that one tiny piece of information is "realized." And then: "Voila!;" or perhaps: "Eureka!;" generally translated as "*I've found it*!"

This can often be the realization that: "A theory that explains or explained nothing, now explains everything." The assumption that someone who is proffering something that seems to make no sense is merely an idiot, is often quite dangerous. Here there is idiocy involved—but it is not necessarily on the part of the "proffer."

There is that old one about the worker, who every day brings a wheelbarrow full of dirt to the security gate. Every day security goes through the dirt, and finding nothing concealed, lets him pass. After a few months of this, it turned out the worker was actually stealing wheelbarrows.

Michelle Obama gained substantial notoriety with her famous statement(s):

> "Barack knows that we are going
> to have to make some sacrifices;
> we are going to have to
> change our conversation;
> we're going to have to change
> our traditions, our history;
> we're going to have to move into a
> different place as a nation."[12.1]

The first two lines could easily represent the type of bromide often heard with the change of any administration.

For example:

> "It's gonna be tough,
> but we'll get through it.
> We'll all have to sacrifice,
> but in the end it will be worth it.
> If we all sacrifice and work together *today*,
> we'll have a better *tomorrow*."

Although this sounds a bit like the trite "highway" used car dealer slogan: "Pay Now - Save Later;" it nevertheless is a fair representation of what is usually proffered by politicians who want to make; at least what are in his or her mind;

positive changes—and usually these words can be fairly described as "innocuous drivel."

But this type of "drivel," is contained only in the first two lines of her statement. A major transition and unusual deviation occurs after the appearance of the word: "conversation."

"We are going to have to change our *conversation*," may just mean that serious issues that had previously been avoided, will now be dealt with. No more: "kicking the can down the road." This administration will correct all of those "third rail" issues, and so these need to be brought into the public discourse—hence changing the *conversation*.

But what follows: "We're going to have to change our traditions, our history; we're going to have to move into a different place as a nation;" makes this benign interpretation extremely unlikely.

Despite any public perceptions to the contrary, Michelle Obama was not merely the Nation's "Personal Trainer and Dietician." Rather; she is an accomplished attorney, and thus likely like any competent attorney, chose her words quite carefully. The appearance of this "change our conversation," thus represented a transition to the second part; which is not the typical "pap."

Why would one want to change one's traditions? What is wrong with our current "traditions?"

The answer is that to the statist, these same traditions represent *interference*. "Interference" can be quite subjective; depending upon precisely what it is that is being interfered with.

The enemy, and all of his or its machinations, represents interference to those who wish to "kibosh," (Hebrew: kâbash), the earth. And those '"kiboshers," to the extent that they are in fact "kiboshing," represent interference to the enemy.

Traditions are the representations of many factors. These include cultural and religious factors—which of course do not comport with statism. Thus in the statists mind, these must be "changed;" with the same, (changed), being either a euphemism or an outright lie.

"Change" in this particular usage, essentially means: the removal, (and destruction), of one thing; and replacing it with something else. Perhaps the word "supplanting" would have been more honest, and more accurate; but also much more inflammatory.

And it must be asked as to precisely how it is that one "changes" one's history? It is inarguably true, that one cannot change the past—at least in the material realm. So then precisely how is it that one can change one's history, if history is considered as a record of the past?

She did not say that we need to change our past, as this position; even for a statist; is not only not possible, but not even a believable or tenable position. Ergo; it is or was the *record* of our past, to which she was referring that must be "changed."

This is not new. Other countries have been doing this precise thing for decades, centuries, and millennia. And even in this country, the term "history revisionists," has been around for quite some time. So she was in fact not proffering anything new. What it seems she was doing that *was* unusual; was attempting "before the fact," to obtain *consent* of the public to engage in changing the *record* of our past.

Although no reliable information regarding the actual source of this quote could be found, possibly it was the philosopher George Santayana who said:

> *"Those who do not learn history*
> *are doomed to repeat it.*[12.2]

This is germane to this very matter. Among other things, history teaches us what others have done when faced with decisions, and what the outcome was. This provides guidance as to what to do or not do when faced with similar situations.

Ideally; "history" represents *knowledge*, and perhaps even a sprinkling of *wisdom*; and proper decision making by the utilization of these truths. Once the superfluities of a seemingly complex or complicated situation are removed, there generally is never anything new that remains.

If *history*; or the *record* of the past can be changed; then current and future decisions based upon this "history" can likewise be changed. Change the record of the past, and one can change the future.

Meteorologist Joe Bastardi, is attributed with the following, (paraphrased): "Ignorance of the past makes one arrogant about the future."

What should the record of the past be changed to? Whatever it is that is required in order to obtain the outcome that the statist currently desires—of course. This represents *manipulation*; and obtaining "desired" decisions, by the utilization of deception. History is then transformed from a *constant*, to a *variable*.

Again this is not new. What is unusual; is the blatant *public* request that we all agree to begin deliberately lying to each other.

The final statement: "We're going to have to move into a different place as a nation;" must necessarily be taken either literally or non-literally.

There is no record of either Michelle Obama, or Barack Obama *suggesting* that perhaps Mexico and/or Central/South America should be annexed to what currently is the United States; and for eight years, there was no record of any *attempts* to do so. Even the blatant "open borders" policy, affects not the "place" where we "move;" but rather the "place" to where illegal aliens can move. So it seems that this was not to be taken literally.

Thus the meaning of "to move into a different place as a nation," is non-literal. Meaning; that the current "place," that we currently "are;" is unacceptable to her. The record of Barack Obama is clear with respect to that desired "place;" and President Trump was the predictable result of these attempts. This is stated with no expression of any opinion regarding President Trump; but rather only the predictability of the response to this attempted "move."

This "place" is the same place other countries have "moved," where the results have been predictably disastrous. Whether the desired destination, or "place," was to be similar to the failing European socialist "utopias;" or an even much more statist oriented platform, is of course left to the observer.

It is not difficult to see yet another failure of the statist "thinking," with respect to Michelle Obama's efforts regarding school lunches. Is there anything wrong with efforts to get children to eat healthy foods? The answer is of course not. But to the statist, once it is decided that students should be eating kale and brown rice for lunch; all that is necessary is to provide students with no other choice, and they will then somehow like eating the same—simply and solely because the statist believes this is so.

Of course this did not work, as school dumpsters were then filled with this same food that the students simply refused to eat. If Michelle had somehow gotten the students to "let on" that these vegetables were pizza, perhaps the results would have been different—but likely not.

But here again, the statist believes that they are not subject to natural law; most particularly that pesky one that "a thing is what it is." The problem, is that even though the statist believes that *they* are not subject to natural law; their "subjects;" here the students; know that *they* are. No matter how many agreed to "let on" that a rutabaga was a calzone, it was still a rutabaga; and they simply refused to eat it.

The statist, just like the enemy, relies upon the *consent* of the victim. This is why it was so important for Michelle to attempt to get enough people to *agree* to: "change our history." Statists;

just like many others, including the enemy; also rely on "exploitation of scruples." This is a means by which upright behavior, is used against the upright. The "relative certainty," that the victim or target will refrain from "telling it like it is" to the statist; is a key weapon of the statist.

This is also precisely why we are told in Proverbs 26:4-5, to never answer a fool in *accord* with his folly; but rather to give the answer that is *deserved* (paraphrased).[12,3]

Sometimes the deserved "answer" is a rebuke, (for a foolish statement); or a reproof (for a foolish behavior). Sometimes the "deserved" answer is simply say or do nothing. And sometimes the "deserved" answer is an outright rejection, with or without any explanation even being provided.

And Proverbs 26:4-5 also tells us why we should not answer a fool in accordance with his folly. The answer is because we will then become like him.

Some maintain that "life" consists of nothing more than a series of decisions. Some also maintain that "wherever" a person finds his or her self in life, this is the sum total of all of his or her previous decisions.

But even without being an absolutist with regard to the first statement; it can be said that H. Sapiens essentially must constantly make decisions—at least while in the wakeful state.

And with respect to the second statement, and the understanding of "equal and opposite reactions;" i.e.; *karma*; there is also substantial truth contained therein.

This is precisely why man is constantly the target of two mutually exclusive forces:

One force is that of God. He promulgates truth, or "that which is." He has given the free will and the authority to H. Sapiens, to make choices. He does not insist that we obey him, but "hopes" that we do. God really has no choice in this, as He has already delegated substantial authority to man. Unless of course God were to sin, which of course is quite impossible.

In furtherance of this, God provides knowledge and wisdom, and asks that we shâmar; or *protect* this knowledge and wisdom as though surrounded by a "hedge of thorns." We are then supposed to utilize this "shâmar-ed" knowledge, in the decision making process.

The other force is that which is *not* of God. He or it promulgates falsehood, or "that which is not." He, (the enemy), knows well of man's free will; and thus the authority granted to H. Sapiens to make choices. He, (the enemy), insists that we obey *him*; but *fears* that we do not.

In furtherance of this, he, (the enemy), provides *falsehood*, and asks that we shâmar or protect these *falsehoods*. These actions by design; are to supplant actual knowledge and wisdom, and he wants us to protect these *falsehoods* as though surrounded by a "hedge of thorns." We are then supposed to utilize these "shâmar-ed" falsehoods, in the decision making process.

As "*second* in charge" in the *overall* "authority department," but "*first* in charge," in at least the earthly "kiboshing" department; H. Sapiens are bombarded by these two forces 24/7—and yes, sometimes while not even conscious.

"Upright" decisions, are those that tend to keep men "upright;" or standing. These decisions are based upon truth from above.

"Non-upright" decisions, are those based upon something other than this truth. The relationship between the meaning of "lie" as an untruth; and the meaning of "lie" as physically being in "non-upright position, (lying down);" is more than coincidental, as one can easily begat the other.

With perhaps only a few exceptions, *upright* H. Sapiens represent a much greater danger to the enemy; than does man in the horizontal, (non-upright), position—both literally and figuratively. But just as in the physical sense, remaining upright in the non-physical sense; requires much more effort than does "lying"—by either definition.

The statist's need for consent of H. Sapiens, represents nothing more than an attempt to *counterfeit* Locke's "Social Contract." "Just laws" are those enacted with the informed consent of the governed. Here the *means* is critical to the "justness" of the law.

"Informed consent" requires information, and falsehood; as opposed to information *about* a falsehood; is not generally considered to be "information." In agreed upon areas, man's individual authority is willfully subrogated to others. But any means utilized other than the truth, cannot be "informed consent;" and thus voids any subsequent subrogation of man's free will.

But statists have their own version of a "Social Contract;" where truth is not only *irrelevant*; but also *non-objective*:

The *irrelevancy*, is because to a statist; it is the acquisition of power by any means possible that is the most important thing. This is because they believe that it is not "what is," that is in any way important; but rather (what they think) *they* are, that provides that which is "just." Statists believe that it is *they* who are responsible for making choices for men, based upon what they, (the statists), think or believe at any given time.

It is the *non-objectivity*, or is *subjectivity*, which forms the basis for the statist's power. This of course then necessarily requires the impossible— immunity to natural law.

This is because when "that which is," (actuality); conflicts with the statist's *reality*; the statist's reality must nevertheless somehow prevail.

But "natural law," requires that one's reality must conform to actuality, and not the reverse—at least in the material realm. When reality and actuality conflict, natural law requires that the results are based upon that which *is*, (actuality); and not which is *perceived*, (reality). One can neither drink nor drown in a desert mirage, no matter what one believes.

This then necessarily leads to the *emotional* prevailing over the *intellectual*. Whether it is the proven logical fallacy of the "Even if it saves just one" "equation(oid);" or it is the impossibility of portions of that which is promulgated by many religions; the commonality is emotion.

"They just have a different viewpoint," represents an insufficient rationale for two plus two equaling five. The First Amendment in guaranteeing free speech; likewise guarantees both the right, as well as the opportunity, to prove that the speaker is a fool.

Being a dual being, man requires two types of nourishment:

Much is made of the requirements of man's physical or material nourishment. Man must consume that which is consistent with the requirements of the physical body, or various forms of "dis-ease" will be the result. Man cannot consume garbage, and yet nevertheless somehow remain healthy. Man cannot consume poisons, and avoid the effect of these poisons simply because he either did not know, or was told they were "good for him." And although there is much controversy regarding precisely what constitutes "healthy food" at any given time; this truth nevertheless remains.

The same is so with the *immaterial* portion of man. Man must take in that which is consistent with his immaterial portion as designed, or the result is also "dis-ease." But here there is generally much less concern or consensus, as to what constitutes "healthy food" for man's immaterial portion. And just as is the case with the poison, man cannot feed his *immaterial* portion with that which is inconsistent with the needs of the same, and yet somehow remain healthy.

Man was *designed*. It is true that man has *evolved* into different colors shapes and sizes; and once it is understood that the original *created* hosts existed likely hundreds of thousands of years before the *formation* of Adam, there is or was ample time for these changes. But these changes largely represent changes only to the *container*, or the *material* portion of man. That which is *formed* has evolved; but that immaterial portion blown or breathed into mans nostrils, has changed little, if at all.

Thus the immaterial part of man, or that which is "blown into his nostrils," when this container becomes "living;" remains essentially the same. This portion is what is designed with free will in mind; and said free will can only be interfered with *justly*.

And it is this immaterial portion of man that is "equal." It would be buffoonery to suggest that the *material* portion of all H. Sapiens are equal to each other; except perhaps in the case of identical twins, or something similar. Even mitotic cell division, does not result in equal daughter cells, as the non-nuclear components are not distributed equally. There is no equal distribution of ribosomes, mitochondria, etc.

The "equal" part of man, is that immaterial part which animates man—the "I am" part.

This immaterial part changes little or not at all with evolution. It comes directly from God at the time of birth. In order for that part which come directly from God to evolve; then the source; God Himself; would likewise have to be "evolving."

This of course is entirely different than God choosing an "I am" that He knows is more suitable for a particular type of "kiboshing," at a particular time. This may appear to be "evolution" of the immaterial part, but is not.

Statists understand none of this.

The very tenets of statism, are antithetical to the design of man's immaterial portion. Thus whenever statist policies are enacted, imbalances are created in the target or victim. And this imbalance represents potential energy which will ultimately be balanced. This is in contradistinction to the enactment of "just" laws.

These imbalances can be individual or collective. They can be short term or long term. The American Revolution falls into the collective long term category. The election of Donald Trump also falls into the collective category, but shorter term.

The *effects* of individual short term imbalances; are often mitigated on an individual basis, by the consumption of "balancing agents." Some of these "balancing agents," can range from alcohol to serious drugs. One problem with these; is that although there may be short term mitigation of the *effects* of these imbalances, the imbalance itself generally remains unchanged by the use of these "agents." Another problem, is that some of these "balancing agents" are quite dangerous.

Whenever "self-medication" is present, one must ask the reason(s) for the same. This has happened throughout the history of man, with the most accepted "balancing agent" being alcohol. When any society begins to experience the utilization of more dangerous substances on a massive scale; one must honestly determine the reason(s) for the same.

There have always been those individuals who consume, or "use," the most dangerous drugs available. Generally this has been due to individual *intrinsic* imbalances, whose effects are being "mitigated." This generally represents an individual problem, which must be addressed individually. Although these individuals have always existed, they have historically represented only a small percentage of the population.

But when the use of these dangerous drugs becomes what is best characterized as an *epidemic*; the imbalances are likely *extrinsic*. Looking into the individual's personal reason(s), then becomes a bit of a fool's errand. When the use of dangerous drugs becomes an epidemic; just as is normally the case with other "epidemics;" it become a matter of not what is *in there*, but rather what is *out there*.

"Out there" can represent the increased availability of dangerous drugs. Since the statists have undertaken "open border" policies in order to attempt to secure the vote for decades to come; they simultaneously and predictably opened the border to the smuggling of these drugs into the US.

But "demand," and "quantity demanded," are not synonymous. "Demand," refers to factors such as taste; while "quantity demanded," refers to price. How many today would wear Nehru jackets, solely because they could be obtained inexpensively? Thus the reduction in prices for these dangerous drugs largely affects the "quantity demanded" for these drugs; and not so much the "demand" for a drug—except perhaps for minors; who today risk suffering dire consequences, for even attempting to obtain more benign "balancing agents."

Out there," can also represent those forces "out there," causing these imbalances. Here this is primarily an issue of "demand;" with price or "cost," (quantity demanded), being only a secondary factor. Often beginning with abuse of prescription opioids; when the "price" becomes "too high;" users then switch to a "less expensive" substitute—all too often heroin. In today's world, one is much more likely to get into trouble for "doctor shopping," than to get into trouble buying illegal drugs. But either way, there is demand.

Although all "drug dealers" should be removed from the public sphere; that is not the answer. And although physicians who overprescribe should be stopped; that is not the answer either.

The only way to stop the problem is to remove the *cause* of the problem. Drug use is a problem in and of itself; but it also represents both signs and symptoms of a much larger problem. And that larger problem; is what it is that influences the matter of *demand*.

The question must be asked as to precisely *why* demand for these substances has increased to these epidemic levels? Again demand here refers to the number of persons choosing to use the drug, and not so much how much of the drug is demanded.

One cannot consummate a business contract, (offer and acceptance); then abrogate major provisions of said contract; and expect no reaction from the other party to this contract. The same is true with a "social contract."

The US government has largely become a corrupt and lawless institution—at least for those in power. As previously mentioned, we have the highest Court in the land, ruling that provisions of a law are a tax and thus are constitutional; after previously indicating that if the very same provision were a tax, the case could not even be heard by them at that time.

We have the FBI director in great detail listing details of illegal behavior, and then usurping the authority of the Justice Department by declining to recommend prosecution.

We have the Ninth Circuit Court issuing absurd political rulings, that are overturned the overwhelming majority of the time. In fact; given this, justice would be better served by dissolving this court, and tossing a coin instead.

The average person realizes that a "two tiered" system is in play; and that is not what they "signed up for." There clearly are different thresholds for those in power, than for the average person with respect to being held accountable for criminal activity. Actions that would result in a long prison term for the average person; absent a political vendetta, often simply do not apply to those in power—and people notice.

Ayn Rand described statist reasoning, as such that one cannot control law abiding citizens, as they do not break the law. Therefore laws must be designed to prohibit that which honest and decent people normally do; and then they can be controlled.

Accomplishing this legislatively is difficult, as legislators are subject to removal. This is why it is "regulations" that are utilized. Here unelected bureaucrats determine behavior via the regulatory scheme; with the former EPA being a prime example. These unelected bureaucrats, determine what it is that the legislators actually meant, or perhaps better phrased; what it is that these bureaucrats *wished* they had meant. Today it seems that no matter what benign behavior one wishes to engage in, there is some law or regulation designed to control it and/or punish them for it.

There is also that which is colloquially referred to as "Sue and Settle." Here, new "policies" are implemented outside of the normal regulatory process. Special interest parties are encouraged to file suit against some part of the federal government. Then instead of fighting the suit; the federal government "settles" the litigation by agreeing to whatever these groups are demanding. Since this is a "settlement;" policies that would never survive the normal regulatory process can then be implemented.

There are tremendous costs involved in implementing these schemes. Outside of the obvious economic costs, there are the psychological and emotional costs to H. Sapiens. To suggest that the US is today a "free country" other than in a relative sense; belies the actuality. We are no longer a free people, unless the meaning of free is changed to actually mean "free-er." US citizens are in fact "more free" than the citizens of any other country; but of course this does not mean free.

Freedom is supposed to be the norm, with any changes to this status requiring a valid "social contract."

Freedom or free, is not supposed to mean that restrictions on freedom in the US are not as bad as some other countries. This is not freedom, but merely a comparison of the restrictions on freedom; and then calling the least amount of restrictions freedom. With this thinking, the US would become "free-er," simply by doing nothing while other countries degrade. So by this same thinking, the simple emergence of Hitler, Tojo, Stalin, etc.; would then have made the US "more free."

When one moves next to an active railroad track, after a while it is often claimed that: "I don't hear it anymore." This may be true, but this in no way means that the noise does not affect them. Neurologically, the inhibition of the "hearing," occurs *after* other neurological pathways. Thus although they may in fact not be conscious of the noise, it nevertheless still affects them.

A similar mechanism is involved with the restrictions on freedom. H. Sapiens are designed to be free. H. Sapiens can *survive* not being free, but as previously stated, imbalances are created. And the magnitude of these imbalances; is reasonably proportional to the amount of freedom taken away. It matters little that the frog was first placed in cold water, and *then* heat was supplied, (political progressivism).

In the case of a *just* "social contract," minor imbalances are created; but these are balanced by practicality. This is the very purpose of the contract.

But as freedom diminishes more and more, these imbalances cannot be balanced by "practicality," for at least two reasons:

Firstly; because there is simply little or no practicality. These freedoms are not taken away to benefit citizens; thus perhaps "stolen" may be the more correct terminology. Unlike a just "social contract," where some degree of freedom is willfully *given* to others; here freedoms are taken away to satisfy the desires of the ruling class.

Each and every time those in the government "cut a deal" that benefits themselves, the citizens do not profit—the citizens lose. These freedoms are taken away, because the "ruling class" believes that it can get away with it—and unfortunately thus far, they have largely been correct.

Secondly; there is a "tipping point," beyond which H. Sapiens cannot properly function. When these imbalances reach a certain level, H. Sapiens *attempt* to find ways to balance these imbalances.

There must be a distinction made between *balancing the actual imbalance*, (cause); and mitigating the personal *effects* of the imbalance.

Mitigating the personal *effects* of the imbalance has at least two manifestations:

One is *personal* and *objective*: "I don't care, they are not getting my 'assault' rifle," or; "I don't care, I am still getting fireworks;" being two examples of the personal *objective*.

Mitigating these *personal* and *objective* effects, can sometimes change the actuality. The state of Georgia, in its wisdom; recently changed their fireworks laws. The fact is, that their prior illegality had only a marginal effect on demand or quantity demanded; and the continual loss of sales tax revenue to South Carolina and Alabama, were likely major factors—whether admitted or not. Here the mitigation of the personal and objective imbalance in fact changed the actuality.

Irrespective of one's opinion of him, attempting to balance *personal* and *objective imbalance*, was a major reason why we have President Trump.

The other is *personal* and *subjective*:

But mitigating these *personal* and *subjective* imbalances; i.e.; the "stresses" involved; is another matter. This is where individuals attempt to balance the emotional, psychological, and other effects of these imbalances; and often by the use of the aforementioned "balancing agents."

Does any reasonable person believe that the statists would change their objectives and goals in any meaningful way simply because of use/overuse/abuse of these "balancing agents?"

Not only does the use of these give the statists more power over the "masses;" but these same "masses" can become much more in need of that which statists proffer and control; as well as becoming more "pliable."

Whether it is the excessive consumption of vodka in the former USSR, or in Russia today; or the epidemic levels of consumption of "recreational" drugs, particularly opioids, in the US today; each is a sign and symptom of a population existing in an intolerable environment.

Does this mean that if the government suddenly became that which was actually *agreed* to in the founding documents, that "recreational" drug use would disappear? Of course not, but it is not merely the *use* of these substances that is the new problem. It is both the *epidemic* levels of use, and the *types* of drugs used, that are the problems.

And today, there is an unusual seeming un-commonality regarding those who utilize these substances. Meaning; that at a minimum there are little or none of the usual demographic similarities in users. It is understood that correlation is not causation; but the reason no "commonality" is apparent, is because of the failure to look in the correct places.

Once the "cause" for a "normal" epidemic is determined; e.g.; smallpox, HIV, etc; then *exposure* becomes the critical factor. Since pathogenic organisms do not "spontaneously generate," exposure to said infectious agent is required. If one is not exposed, one simply cannot contract that particular disease.

Much to the chagrin of some "religious folks;" the fact is that the original HIV/AIDS epidemic had nothing whatsoever to do with homosexuality directly. It was the *lifestyle* of some homosexuals at that time, which increased *exposure* to the virus that was the problem.

The present drug epidemic has a cause which affects that "*equal*" (immaterial) part of man somewhat *equally*—which is why none of the usual demographics are particularly reliable predictives.

Thus the cause appears to be *omnipresent*, and there is a *commonality* of susceptibility. All men are designed to be free; and all in the US, (with the exception of the "ruling class"); must live in the same environment, where one's rights have been and continue to be systematically removed. And this is done for reason(s) that do not comport with any agreed upon "social contract" arrangement.

This goes against the very design of that immaterial part of man; and in fact, goes against the wishes of man's Creator.

And the outright lying to young people about the dangers of "drugs" did not help matters. It is true that all drug users and addicts begin with either mother's milk, or formula. But young people were not taught that.

Instead; they were taught that tobacco and alcohol would unquestionably lead them down the road to drug use. When this turned out to be false, many questioned the veracity of the remainder of the "teachings." This is why drug use among those completing these programs is often reported to actually be significantly greater than those "ignorant folk." No one questions the intentions of those that offered these programs. Rather it was lack of sound judgment, combined with personal biases.

To the non-alcoholic, alcohol is something that is to be used responsibly.

To the "normal" alcoholic, alcohol must be avoided, but it is understood that it is *they* who are the major problem, and it is *they* who must change—else the substitution of alcohol with some other intoxicating substance is a serious risk.

To the "dry alcoholic," it is the alcohol that is the problem. There is nothing they need to change about themselves, except to avoid alcohol. Therefore there is no such thing as the responsible use of alcohol for anyone. It is easier to dismiss the responsible use of alcohol worldwide for millennia, than it is to admit one's personal faults. [It seems that this was tried for a while with the 18th Amendment; and except perhaps for organized crime, this did not work out very well.]

Generally, when behavior "far outside the norms," such as the current drug epidemic, is observed; it is generally for one of two reasons:

The *first* reason has to do with the *individual*. For whatever reasons(s), the *individual's* environment is being perceived incorrectly. Thus the behavior(s) are the result of a reality, (perception); which is inconsistent with the actuality. Here it is the case that they are in fact not "out to get him," any personal beliefs notwithstanding. Thus here it is the individual that must change. This is a *reality* based matter;

and trained professionals can often assist in this change.

The *second* reason has to do with the *environment* in which individuals exist. These bizarre behaviors are consistent with "normal" reactions; but here reactions to an intolerable *environment*. The refusal to admit this changes nothing. One can either deliberately, or through genuine ignorance, fail to see the true causative factors; yet they nevertheless persist. This is an *actuality* based matter; and these same trained professionals cannot change this environment.

The only way "this one" can be remedied, is to change the environment. But since the causative environment has been moving in this loss of freedom direction at least since the time of Woodrow Wilson, this represents a difficult undertaking.

In addition, it is a bit like root beer. Few under the age of fifty know what real root beer, (soft drink), tastes like. What is currently proffered as "root beer," has little resemblance to the actual product. Most of those who drink today's root beer know nothing else, and think that this is root beer.

The same can be said for freedom. Placing handcuffs on a citizen at a traffic stop while being told; "you are not being arrested, just detained;" is absurd.

The word "arrest" generally means to *stop*; as in "cardiac arrest." Stop what? Here it means to *stop* an individual from exercising his free will. A "traffic stop;" AKA: being "pulled over;" technically is in fact an arrest; in that the driver and occupants are prevented from travelling freely. Absent "legal authority," this could be considered as kidnapping in many jurisdictions.

Those who are then placed in handcuffs at a traffic stop because of "possible probable cause," think that this is what freedom tastes like, because they are "used to it."

And the police officers involved, do not see anything any differently. Perhaps this is an outgrowth of the idea of it being better to be "tried by twelve than carried by six"—an idea which tends to lose its appeal long before the trial even begins.

So we have developed various "euphemisms," for these various degrees of "arrests:"

When a car is "stopped" this is a "traffic stop" and not an arrest— even though arrest means to stop.

When handcuffs are placed on an individual, today this is not called an arrest, but rather merely a "detention"—as though the "stop" itself which had already detained the driver and passengers, was somehow not already a detention.

It is only when the individual is removed from the scene under duress, that the term "arrest" is finally admitted.

The truth is that the stop, in and of itself, in fact literally represents the arrest and/or detention.

The placement of handcuffs on a citizen is not accurately described as "detained," but in fact is actually "restrained."

And when "the individual is removed from the scene under duress," this would then be better characterized as "charged;" as the arrest/detention, as well as the restraining have already occurred.

And what about "warrants?" Good luck to the admissibility of any "evidence" obtained by any law enforcement officer; who against the wishes of the owner; insists upon conducting a search of a premises, merely *claiming* that a "search warrant" exists, or is "on its way."

Yet if the live law enforcement television programs are in any way an accurate representation; it seems that on a routine basis, citizens are "arrested," after merely *told* that there exists a warrant requiring the same.

Should the citizen object, and demand immediate proof of the existence of said warrant; he or she would likely be charged with the crime of "resisting arrest." It seems that they often must wait until some point *after* they are "taken away," to be provided with physical proof of the authority which authorized this action—and of course there can always be, and in fact are errors.

Why is there a difference?

One answer; is because normally, the *evidence* from any unauthorized or *unjust* search would likely be useless in a court of law. And the commission of said unauthorized "search," would at a minimum be civilly actionable; and may in and of itself constitute a crime such as larceny, or even burglary. It is only that "just" authority; (the warrant); that provides the separation.

But the routine unconstitutional interfering with the freedom and dignity of citizens, seems to have much higher threshold; (good faith); for any civil or criminal repercussions. Thus it seem these current rules and practices are much more concerned with the welfare of law enforcement; rather than the freedoms of the citizens they are sworn to protect and serve. Although this is understandable, it is far from "just."

None of this is in any way meant as any type of slur on law enforcement. They have an extremely dangerous job protecting citizens; and any reasonable person is thankful for this, and supports them. But this is no way provides any license to *label* a thing or things other than what *it* is or *they* are. This practice is the statist method.

Why is it this way? Again; in order to provide maximum possible protection to law enforcement officers. After all, if the routine violations of the rights of millions of citizens; by routinely handcuffing, (restraining), these same millions of thus far criminally innocent citizens during traffic stops, has even the most incredibly infinitesimally remote chance of even possibly "saving just one;" it is worth it, and a small price to pay—isn't it?

And the "reclassification" or "renaming," (euphemism), of these various police actions, is nothing more than an attempt to alter the reality of an unacceptable *actuality*, to a *reality*, (perception), which is "acceptable" to the victims.

Then there is the interrogation of one who may merely and unknowingly have a faulty tail light bulb. After the initial: "Where are your papers?," (German accent deliberately omitted); it then becomes the: "Where have you been? Where are you going?;" etc. It is unclear how these intrusions in any way comport with the Constitution and due process.

It is also unclear if citizens; unlike those who work for the citizens; have any type of Constitutional, or "just" legal requirement to at all times maintain on their person evidence of: "who they are."

Despite this; after "nine eleven," the statists and many purported non-statists, made the determination that nevertheless this was in fact so. The federal government determined that a national registry of individuals was now required. But either because of the illegality; or because of lack of courage to enact the statist's incessantly desired national registry; the federal government "passed the buck" to the states.

So instead of taking both the legal and political risks of creating a national registry, the states essentially were forced to do this on behalf of the federal government. And what was chosen for this was an *inelastic* entity—the driver's license. This is precisely why obtaining or renewing a driver's license suddenly became a debacle.

Thus we now have not a true federal registry, but rather interlinked state identification registries, serving the very same purposes. Had they chosen an *elastic* entity in the enactment of this scheme, it would not have worked.

Now it is virtually impossible to live without this means of identification, which of course was the desired result. And it does not require much of a "stretch," for those in power; those who are supposed to *serve* citizens; to extrapolate the simple unwillingness or inability to provide these "papers," into evidence of at best *negligence*, or even *criminality*.

Today, should an otherwise lawful citizen be unable to provide these "papers" on demand at any place or time; said "negligence or even criminality" is often *presumed*. It is unclear whether or not this is worse than the use of Social Security numbers for identification, when "Not To Be Used For Identification" appears; or at least used to appear; on the bottom of all Social Security cards.

And it is also a troublesome fact, that those who have the actual power (citizens); can be held criminally liable; e.g.; charged with a felony; if they lie to those to whom these same citizens have subrogated portions of said power. Wherein lies the function of "under oath," if it is already a crime to lie to certain individuals while *not* "under oath?"

Yet these same "subrogatees," are free to lie, to spin yarns "from whole cloth," to these same citizens at will; with little or no consequence. And the Courts have upheld the legality of law enforcement routinely lying to the citizenry.

It is interesting to note how the thus far successful attempts to have a federal police force, somehow comport with the 10th Amendment to the US Constitution. The overwhelming argument; is that police power is reserved for the states, and thus the federal government is barred from maintaining any type of police force.

So the answer was to "let on" that this federal police force is not any type of police force at all, but rather is merely a "bureau."

And since this is only a bureau, this bureau is thus not *directly* involved in police/law enforcement matters, which remain reserved for the states; but rather is only involved *tangentially*, via "investigations."

So as long as all agree to "let on" that this is merely a "bureau," and not a police force; and that it is not actually involved with law enforcement, but rather only with "investigations;" it can thus also be "let on" that all remains in compliance with the US Constitution.

And since this is not called a police force but rather a *bureau*; those individuals directly involved in these investigations, are not to be called police officers, but rather *agents*. This is required in order to maintain this farce of purported constitutionality.

The FBI is a highly professional organization, with highly trained and extremely dedicated employees. The FBI is an outstanding organization, and its work product far excels any similar organization anywhere in the world. But none of this relates to the point.

The problem is *not* that they are not a highly efficient and professional organization. The problem is *not* so much that much of what they do is *ultra-vires*, or *without* authority. The problem, is that the "smart money" bets on it being such; that most of their activities are not merely without "just" authority; but are clearly *prohibited* by the US Constitution.

But there was at one time a *need* to solve a purported problem caused by the incredible amounts of wealth and power accumulated by certain groups of individuals. And much of this accumulation was the direct and predictable result of yet another governmental overreach— *prohibition.*

Citizens must "understand" that this is all "necessary," because we live in a world of crime and terrorism. Consequently; if one objects to these types of actions, then one must necessarily be hiding something. Citizens should "cheerfully" accept these incessant intrusions, and be thankful.

The human desire for; and/or the exercise of the constitutionally guaranteed rights of privacy, has now become at a minimum "probable cause;" and in some areas "clear and convincing evidence;" of guilt with regard to some unspecified crime or crimes. Once again, this is in no way to be construed as any type of slur against law enforcement, as with very few exceptions they play by the rules. It is the *rules*, and not law enforcement that are the cause of the problem.

The amount of criminal activity related *directly* and *indirectly* to drugs is staggering. This not only includes drug trafficking, but also to the crimes committed in order to pay the drug dealers. In addition, there are the crimes committed as the result of drug influenced "judgment."

Clearly the "war on drugs" has been lost. There is that old one about the first thing to do when one finds one's self in a hole—stop digging. It is sadly ironic that the government's answer to today's epidemic level drug problem which they are largely responsible for creating; is more governmental intrusion into people's lives. Again, there have always been drug users and associated deaths; but never in the history of the US, did they exist to the extent seen today. But of course in the overall sense, never has the US been less free than it is today.

And to the limited extent that this "terrorism" argument may have any merit; this likewise proves to this very same extent, the failure of the US government to adequately address the terrorism issue. Thus the "sacrificial part" or "what has to give" are the freedoms of US citizens—as instead of destroying the causes; i.e.; *the terrorists themselves*; the policy is to merely try and prevent terrorist *actions*.

The correct policy should be to have more concern for the rights of US citizens, than for the rights of other countries; particularly those countries that choose to harbor terrorists.

It should be a matter of US policy, that any terrorist anywhere in the world chooses a death sentence when he or she chooses terrorism. When "actionable intelligence" exists with respect to the presence of terrorists anywhere in the world, swift and decisive action should be undertaken. It is *other countries* who must "understand" that this is all "necessary," because we live in a world of terrorism.

To be clear; this means the immediate destruction of any terrorist stronghold discovered anywhere in the world. Once "actionable intelligence" exists, then the stronghold is immediately destroyed.

Those countries that harbor, and thus aid and abet terrorists, should learn to expect this as the predictable price for their actions. And those countries who do not harbor terrorists should thank us. This is nothing new. It is merely the practical enactment of: "The Bush Doctrine—you are either with us or against us." Or alternatively; "The Bush Doctrine," plus chutzpah.

Those in power should learn to protect the rights of US citizens, and not worry so much about the rights of those countries who are "against us." But infringing upon the rights of US citizens is much easier, and will remain easier—unless and until US citizens increase the costs.

Free societies have potential risks. Police states do not. One cannot have both. This "pendulum," has swung back and forth for many years. One can have a higher degree of security, or a higher degree of freedom. It depends upon which a society values more.

———————

In today's world, politics is everywhere. One cannot attend a musical event or football game, without either hearing someone whose expertise is in an entirely different area; bloviate about some political matter, or seeing some type of action based upon some political viewpoint.

Is it that these are simply unaware of Col. Tom Parker's advice to Elvis about politics? "(Paraphrased) No matter what you state about politics, you will alienate half of your fans." Elvis' response to political questions generally was: "I am just an entertainer."

Or is it that they simply do not care?

Many choose to conflate the exercise of the 1st Amendment *rights* of these citizen's, with the *wisdom* of the same. No sane person argues another individual's right to self-expression. But these expressions can have serious consequences.

There is no constitutional right that forces another to not think that said "bloviator" is a "jerk," (see Jeb Bush on Donald Trump); for inappropriate 1st amendment expressions. And as the Colonel knew quite well, in a free market economy this particular lack of wisdom can be disastrous.

To the extent that these protestations have anything to do with actualities, there are venues available for the same that are much more appropriate. "Appropriate" here meaning without the appearance of: "*I did something for the worst possible reason; just because I could.*" The issue here is not in any way one of *rights*; but rather one that is concerned with *ethics*.

The reasons that today politics is everywhere; are largely two:

The *first* is simply ignorance of the true structure and function of our government.

The *second* is because the statists are *incapable* of evaluating *actualities* in a manner which results in *realities* consistent with the same, unless the actuality is to their liking.

To the statist, the presidential election results of 2016 quite simply cannot be what they are, simply because the statists thought, and continue to think otherwise. Thus to the statist, it is inarguable there *must* exist reasons why the "apparent winner," is not legitimate—and it is simply a matter of discovering, (dis-covering) these reasons.

This discovering or uncovering, presupposes the existence of a thing that is "covered." Ergo; it is a given that: "What happened," was an illegitimate election; because the "apparent outcome," did not ever exist in the statists reality, and thus could not possibly represent an actuality.

This "Trump Derangement Syndrome," would have been predictable to anyone who understands the statist mentality. Statists must keep politics everywhere, in order to maximize the level of success in changing the realities of the citizenry from *actuality* based realities, to realities that instead are based upon the statist's *non-actuality* based *reality*.

The statists have slowly been gaining power for over a century. To them, it is simply impossible that someone who has essentially pledged to undo as much of the "statistocracy;" (author's terminology); as he can in the next 4 – 8 years, could have possibly won against their beliefs and wishes.

This is why much of the "media" was reasonably kind to Donald Trump during the primaries. The media wanted him to win the nomination, because they, (as well as many Republicans); were certain he would lose the election. But once the primaries were over and he was the candidate; "the gloves came off."

In Isaac Asimov's *"Foundation"* series, there is that which is known as "the *mule*." The mule was a man who "came out of nowhere," and began to consolidate power by taking over planets one by one—some without even a battle.

The emergence of the "mule" was not predicted, or even *predictable* to the "Second Foundationers;"—those who were in charge of the "Seldon Plan"—and the means by which the current 1000 year period of chaos would be shortened. The emergence of this mule altered their trajectory substantially. It is only because he was "defanged," that the plan could be slowly recovered.

Donald Trump is the statists' "mule;" or perhaps *anti-mule* is a more accurate term. Anti-mule is more accurate because statists are, and have been involved in activities similar to those of the mule; albeit with somewhat different, but not completely different methods.

And it is Donald Trump that is more analogous to the Second Foundation; i.e.; trying to shorten the period of time that the US is "less great" than it can or should be. Thus the statists need to find some means to "defang" the president. And their willing accomplices in the media, provide a constant barrage of that which would otherwise be considered as nonsensical, and thus not even newsworthy.

What *will* statists control? Whatever they *can* control. If they *can*, (are able to), control it; then they *will* control it—no matter what "it" represents.

There is no discretion involved. What can they control? Whatever they are permitted to control.

Utilizing *truth* in obtaining said permission, is not necessary to the statist. The statist is concerned only with *ends*. The only requirement for justifying *means* is efficacy—will it work?

Benjamin Franklin is attributed with saying: "Those who, (would or can), give up essential liberty; to, (obtain or purchase), a little temporary safety; deserve neither liberty nor safety." The key here is "give up." Citizens often cannot lawfully stop the usurpations of their authority, and the removal of their rights by governmental entities.

But this does not mean that it should be accepted; i.e.; *permitted* to continue. The only *just* authority any governmental agency possesses, is that which has been granted to them by the citizenry; as this authority ultimately resides in the citizenry.

When too much is taken, the citizens not only have a right, but a duty to restore this balance to that which they permit. Unless the Constitutional *structure* of the US government is justly changed, this Constitutional republic remains the system under which we have all agreed to live.

In today's world, those who with respect to our *freedom*, are in favor of "extreme measures," (euphemism), in seeking *security*; find much common ground with the statists in terms of policy, albeit with (hopefully) entirely different motives. But it must be asked if the *reasons* for rights removal in any significant way alter the *effects* of these same rights removal on the citizenry?

Statists love the war on terror. They can now obtain the very same powers they always desired; but now with the *assistance* of those very same persons who would have adamantly opposed them just a short time ago.

To this same extent, to suggest that American's lives and freedoms have not been adversely, and perhaps even irreparably, damaged by this war on terror; would be delusional.

Laws such as the Foreign Intelligence Surveillance Act (FISA), and its offspring the secret Foreign Intelligence Surveillance Court; represent nothing less than the "gun on the mantle" in the "first act." It seems beyond naive to have ever thought that this gun would not be used in a subsequent "act;" and citizens are only now beginning to see the results.

There are mechanisms for lawful restoration of that which has essentially been stolen from the citizenry. These mechanisms; and these mechanisms *only*, should be utilized to correct all these imbalances.

Simply because others; including certain members of the US Supreme Court, are *able*; (as was by his own admission President Clinton); to misuse their "power" to make changes to their liking, does not make these changes "just." The US Constitution has a mechanism for change, and thus does not require their fanciful and *unjust* interpretations.

Supreme Court Judge Anton Scalia was reputed to have had a sign in his office which read: "Stupid But Constitutional." Other members of SCOTUS should likewise have signs, but these should read: "Smart But Unconstitutional." But unlike Justice Scalia, these Justices either do not realize, or simply do not care; that their "just" powers only relate to the latter, (constitutionality); and *never* the former, ("stupid" or "smart"). And even this requires agreement with both the decision, and the long term consequences of *Marbury v. Madison*—a position not universally held.

Prior to his swearing in, Supreme Court Justice Gorsuch said: "A judge who likes every outcome he reaches is very likely a bad judge, stretching for results he prefers rather than those the law demands."

This is a wise admonition to any and all judges who decide any case based upon what *they* believe is "smart" or stupid." Justice Scalia well knew that his duty was not to make any decision based upon what he thought was smart, or that what he "liked;" but only upon the constitutionality of the matter(s) before him.

Other justices are much more concerned with rendering decisions in accordance with what they "like;" AKA: "is smart," (to them);" thereby becoming involved with *policy* matters rather than *constitutionality*—the latter being at best all that *Marbury v. Madison* empowers them to do.

Thus they stand in stark violation of another Gorsuch principle: "It is the role of judges to apply, not alter, the work of the people's representatives."

But in order for correction, all of these current problems must be *recognized* and clearly *identified*. This is the main reason for the obfuscation by so many, and at so many levels.

In one of his novels, Robert Heinlein once wrote a response to a statement by a character who indicated that they do not pay much attention to politics. His response was, (paraphrased): "That they *should* pay attention, as their very life may depend upon it."—JBW

Statists Saving One

Statists Saving One

Glossary

ʻâphâr "(6083) (H) from 6080; *dust* (as *powdered* or *gray*); hence *clay, earth, mud*: - ashes, dust, earth, ground, morter, powder, rubbish." "6080 aphar a prim. root; mean. either to *be gray* or perh. rather to *pulverize*; used only as denom. from 6083, to *be dust*: - cast [dust]]."[G1]

bârâ' "1254 bârâ', a prim. root; (absol.) to create; (qualified) to cut down (a wood), select, feed (as formative processes): - choose, create (creator), cut down, dispatch, do, make (fat)."[G2] "The verb expresses creation out of nothing..."[G3]

charis; "(5485) (G) from 5463; *graciousness* (as *gratifying*), of manner or act..."[10.2]

dia; "(1223) (G) a prim. prep. denoting a *channel* of an act; *through* (in very wide applications..."[10.3]

dunamis "(1411) (G), from 1410; *force* (lit. or fig.); spec. miraculous *power* (usually by impl. a *miracle* itself): - ability, abundance, meaning, might (-ily, - y, -y deed), (worker of) miracle (-s), power, strength, violence, mighty (wonderful) work."[G4]

dynamikós (G) Greek dynamikós powerful, from dýnamis power, from dýnasthai be able, have power; of uncertain origin; ..."

ĕlĕŏs; "(1656) (G) of uncert. affin.; compassion (human or divine espec. active)"[10.8]

ĕrgŏn; "(2041) (G) from a prim. (but obsol.) ĕrgō (to *work*); to *toil* (as an effort or occupation) by impl. an act."[10.4]

frabjous "wonderful, elegant, superb, or delicious."[G6]

gan "(1588) (H) from 1598; a *garden* (as *fenced*): - garden. 1598
ganan a prim. root; to *hedge* about, i.e. (gen.) *protect*: - defend"[9C]

gart "enclosure"

kâbash; "(3533) (H) a prim. root; to *tread* down; hence neg. to *disregard*; pos. to *conquer*, *subjugate*, *violate*: - bring into bondage, force, keep under, subdue, bring into subjection."[1B]

kauchaŏmai; (2744) (G) from some (obsol.) base akin to that of auchĕō (to *boast*) and 2172; to *vaunt* (in a good or bad sense)..."[10.6]

mâlê'; "(4390) or mâlâ' (H)(Esth. 7:5),; a prim. root, to *fill* or (intrans.) *be full* of, in a wide application (lit. and fig.)..."[1A]

MeekRaker   "(Walker/Quadrakoff) any device used to separate the teachable from the non-teachable, by the use of inarguable facts." [G8]

nâchâsh "(5175) (H) nâchâsh, from 5172; a *snake* (from its *hiss*); - serpent."   5172 nachash a prim. root; prop. to *hiss*, i.e. *whisper* a (magic) spell; gen. to *prognosticate*: - x certainly, divine, enchanter, (use) x enchantment, learn by experience, x indeed, diligently observe."[5.8]

nata "(5193) (H) a prim. root; prop. to *strike* in, i.e. *fix*; spec. to *plant* (lit. or fig.): - fastened, plant (-er)."[9E]

polluere "to soil, defile contaminate..."[8.1]

râdâh; "(7287) (H) to *tread* down, i.e. *subjugate*; spec. to *crumble* of: - (come to make to) have dominion, prevail against, reign, (bear, make to) rule, (-r, over), take."[1C]

retrophesy "(Walker/Quadrakoff) like "prophesy" but stating factual knowledge about *past* events, rather than future events."[G9]

tsâbâ' "(6635) (H) or ts^{e}ba'ah, from 6633; a *mass* of persons (or fig. things), espec. reg. organized for war (an *army*); by impl. a *campaign*, lit. or fig.

(spec. *hardship, worship):* - appointed time, (+) army, (+) battle, company, host, service, soldiers, waiting upon, war (-fare). 6633 tsaba a prim. root; to *mass* (an army or servants): - assemble, fight, perform, muster, wait upon, war."[5.6]

yom "(3117) (H)or yôwm, from an unused root mean. To be hot: a day (as the warm hours) whether lit. (from sunrise to sunset, or from one sunset to the next), or fig. (a space of time defined by an associated term) -age,... season..."[9.6]

Bibliography

Chapter 1

1.1 *King James Bible* (Gen. 1:28)
1.2 Walker, J. Bartholomew, *Shâmar to Sharia* © 2016
    Quadrakoff Publications Group, LLC, Wilmington DE
    pp. 8
1.3 United States *Declaration of Independence*
1.4 Walker, J. Bartholomew, *The Emmanic Principles* © 2017
    Quadrakoff Publications Group, LLC, Wilmington DE
1.5 Fifth Amendment to the United States Constitution
1.6 Walker, J. Bartholomew, *The Emmanic Principles* © 2017
    Quadrakoff Publications Group, LLC, Wilmington DE
1.7 Madison, James, retrieved 10/17
    https://www.brainyquote.com/quotes/quotes/j/jamesma
    dis165978.html

Chapter 1 (Embedded)

1A Strong, James. Strong's Exhaustive Concordance of the
    Bible. © 1890 James Strong, Madison, NJ p. 66 (Hebrew)
1B Strong, James. Strong's Exhaustive Concordance of the
    Bible. © 1890 James Strong, Madison, NJ p. 54 (Hebrew)
1C Strong, James. Strong's Exhaustive Concordance of the
    Bible. © 1890 James Strong, Madison, NJ p. 107 (Hebrew)

Chapter 2

2.1 Popper, Karl, retrieved 10/17
    http://www.azquotes.com/quote/687394
2.2 Popper, Karl, retrieved 10/17
    https://www.brainyquote.com/quotes/quotes/k/karlpop
    per159604.htmlhttp://www.azquotes.com/quote/687394

Chapter 3

3.1 Madison, James, Federalist 51, retrieved 10/17
    http://www.constitution.org/fed/federa51.htm
3.2 Brin, David, retrieved 5/17
    http://www.searchquotes.com/quotation/It_is_s
    aid_that_power_corrupts%2C_but_actually_it%
    27s_more_true_that_power_attracts_the_corrup
    tible._The/234441/
3.3 Walker, J. Bartholomew, *Shâmar to Sharia* © 2016
    Quadrakoff Publications Group, LLC, Wilmington DE
    pp. 18
3.4 Madison James, retrieved 5/7
    http://www.constitution.org/jm/jm_quotes.htm
)
3.5 Churchill Winston, retrieved 10/17
    http://www.winstonchurchill.org/resources/quotations/1
    35-quotes-falsely-attributed
3.6 Merriam Webster retrieved 6/17 http://www.merriam-
    webster.com/dictionary/statist
3.7 http://www.merriam-webster.com/dictionary/statism
3.8 Conservapedia retrieved 5/17
    http://www.conservapedia.com/Statism
3.9 Walker, J. Bartholomew, *Shâmar to Sharia* © 2016
    Quadrakoff Publications Group, LLC, Wilmington DE
    pp. 15
3.10 Walker, J. Bartholomew, *Shâmar to Sharia* © 2016
    Quadrakoff Publications Group, LLC, Wilmington DE
    pp. 19
3.11 *King James Bible* (1 Corinthians 8:9)

Bibliography

Chapter 4

4.1 *King James Bible* (Genesis 2:7)
4.2 etymology online retrieved 5/17
   http://www.etymonline.com/index.php?term=moral
4.3 etymology online retrieved 5/17
   http://etymonline.com/index.php?term=sovereign&allowe
   d_in_frame=0
4.4 Walker, J. Bartholomew, *The Emmanic Principles* © 2017
   Quadrakoff Publications Group, LLC, Wilmington DE
4.5 Madison, James, retrieved 5/17
   http://files.libertyfund.org/pll/quotes/180.html
4.6 Walker, J. Bartholomew, Quadrakoff Emma B., *MeekRaker
   Beginnings...* © 2016 Quadrakoff Publications Group, LLC,
   Wilmington DE
4.7 *King James Bible* (Job 1:10-12)
4.8 William Jefferson Clinton retrieved 5/17
   https://www.cbsnews.com/news/bill-clinton-his-life/

Chapter 5

5.1 *Interlinear Bible Hebrew Greek English, 1 Volume edition.* ©
   1976, 1977, 1978, 1979, 1980, 1981, 1984. Second Edition, ©
   1986 Jay P. Green, Sr., Hendrickson Publishers (Genesis 1:2)
   p. 1
5.2 *King James Bible* (Revelation 12:7-9)
5.3 *King James Bible* (Isaiah 14:12)
5.4 *King James Bible* (Luke 10:18-20)
5.5 Walker, J. Bartholomew, Quadrakoff Emma B., *MeekRaker
   Beginnings...* © 2016 Quadrakoff Publications Group, LLC,
   Wilmington DE p. 11
5.6 Strong, James. *Strong's Exhaustive Concordance of the Bible.*
   © 1890 James Strong, Madison, NJ p. 98
5.7 *King James Bible* (Romans 3:23)
5.8 Strong, James. *Strong's Exhaustive Concordance of the Bible.*
   © 1890 James Strong, Madison, NJ p. 78
5.9 *King James Bible* (John 14:12)

Chapter 6

6.1 Shaw, George Bernard, retrieved 5/17,
     http://www.azquotes.com/quote/600281
6.2 Shaw, George Bernard, retrieved 5/17
     http://www.azquotes.com/quote/600282
6.3 Reagan, Ronald, retrieved 5/17
     http://www.newyorker.com/magazine/2009/09/07/kenned
     y-care

Chapter 7

7.1 Fearnow, Benjamin, retrieved 5/17
     http://atlanta.cbslocal.com/2014/02/03/study-hand-smoke-
     exposure-as-deadly-as-smoking/
7.2 Gore, Al, retrieved 5/17 http://freedomkeys.com/gore.htm
7.3 National Cancer Institute, retrieved 5/17
     https://www.cancer.gov/about-cancer/causes-
     prevention/risk/diet/cooked-meats-fact-sheet
7.4 Oak Ridge National Laboratory, retrieved 5/17
     http://fipr.state.fl.us/wp-content/uploads/2014/12/05-DFP-
     015Final.pdf
7.5 Oak Ridge National Laboratory, retrieved 5/17
     http://fipr.state.fl.us/wp-content/uploads/2014/12/05-DFP-
     015Final.pdf

Chapter 8

8.1 Etymology Online, retrieved 5/17
     etymonline.com/index.php?term=pollution
8.2 US Environmental Protection Agency, retrieved 2/17
     epa.gov/ghgemissions/overview-greenhouse-gases
8.3 NASA, retrieved 2/17 climate.nasa.gov/causes/
8.4 US Environmental Protection Agency, retrieved 2/17
     epa.gov/climate-change-science/causes-climate-change
8.5 US Environmental Protection Agency, retrieved 2/17
     epa.gov/climate-change-science/causes-climate-change
8.6 US Environmental Protection Agency, retrieved 2/17
     epa.gov/climate-change-science/causes-climate-change

8.7 NASA, retrieved 2/17 climate.nasa.gov

8.8 NASA, retrieved 2/17 climate.nasa.gov/evidence/

8.9 US Environmental Protection Agency, retrieved 2/17
epa.gov/climate-change-science/causes-climate-change

8.10 US Environmental Protection Agency, retrieved 7/17
epa.gov/climate-change-science/causes-climate-change

8.11 "Climate Change 2013: The Physical Science Basis.
Contribution of Working Group I to the Fifth
Assessment Report of the Intergovernmental Panel on
Climate Change."

8.12 Intergovernmental Panel on Climate Change retrieved 2/17
ipcc.ch/organization/organization.shtml

8.13 Forbes magazine, retrieved 2/17
forbes.com/sites/realspin/2014/03/31/the-ipccs-
latest-report-deliberately-excludes-and-
misrepresents-important –climate –
science/#108695c15097

8.14 Forbes magazine, retrieved 2/17
forbes.com/sites/realspin/2014/03/31/the-ipccs-latest-
report-deliberately-excludes-and-misrepresents-
important –climate –science/#108695c15097

8.15 Forbes magazine, retrieved 2/17
forbes.com/sites/realspin/2014/03/31/the-ipccs-
latest-report-deliberately-excludes-and-
misrepresents-important –climate –
science/#108695c15097)

8.16 retrieved 5/17
cruz.senate.gov/files/documents/Letters/20160526_Clim
ate Change Letter.pdf

8.17 Emanuel, Rahm, retrieved 2/17
brainyquote.com/quotes/quotes/r/rahmemanue409199.
html

Chapter 9

9.1 Rand, Ayn retrieved 5/17 azquotes.com/quote/825505

9.2 Walker, J. Bartholomew, Quadrakoff Emma B., *MeekRaker
Beginnings...* © 2016 Quadrakoff Publications Group, LLC,
Wilmington DE p. 4-6

9.3 *New American Standard Bible*: 1995 update. 1995 (Revelation
12:7-9) The Lockman Foundation: Lahabra, CA

9.4 Walker, J. Bartholomew, Quadrakoff Emma B., *MeekRaker Beginnings...* © 2016 Quadrakoff Publications Group, LLC, Wilmington DE p.

9.5 Walker, J. Bartholomew, Quadrakoff Emma B., *MeekRaker Beginnings...* © 2016 Quadrakoff Publications Group, LLC, Wilmington DE p.

9.6 Strong, James. *Strong's Exhaustive Concordance of the Bible*. © 1890 James Strong, Madison, NJ p. 48 (Hebrew)

9.7 *New American Standard Bible*: 1995 update. 1995 (Gen. 2:8) The Lockman Foundation: Lahabra, CA

9.8 Walker, J. Bartholomew, Quadrakoff Emma B., *MeekRaker Beginnings...* © 2016 Quadrakoff Publications Group, LLC, Wilmington DE p. 66-67

Chapter 9 (Embedded)

9A *Interlinear Bible* (Genesis 1:2) Scripture4all.org

9B *New American Standard Bible*: 1995 update. 1995 (1 Peter 5:8) The Lockman Foundation: Lahabra, CA *Interlinear* version on *Scripture4all.org*

9C Strong, James. *Strong's Exhaustive Concordance of the Bible*. © 1890 James Strong, Madison, NJ p. 28 (Hebrew)

9D *Chambers Dictionary of Etymology*. Copyright © 1988 The H. W. Wilson Company, New York, NY p.422

9E Strong, James. *Strong's Exhaustive Concordance of the Bible*. © 1890 James Strong, Madison, NJ p. 78 (Hebrew)

Chapter 10

10.1 *King James Bible* (Ephesians 2:8-9)

10.2 Strong, James. *Strong's Exhaustive Concordance of the Bible*. © 1890 James Strong, Madison, NJ p. 77 (Greek)

10.3 Strong, James. *Strong's Exhaustive Concordance of the Bible*. © 1890 James Strong, Madison, NJ p. 22 (Greek)

10.4 Strong, James. *Strong's Exhaustive Concordance of the Bible*. © 1890 James Strong, Madison, NJ p. 32 (Greek)

10.5 Dean, Dizzy retrieved 5/17 https://www.brainyquote.com/quotes/quotes/d/dizzydean379853.html)

10.6 Strong, James. *Strong's Exhaustive Concordance of the Bible.*
© 1890 James Strong, Madison, NJ p. 41 (Greek)
10.7 *King James Bible* (Ephesians 2:4)
10.8 Strong, James. *Strong's Exhaustive Concordance of the Bible.*
© 1890 James Strong, Madison, NJ p. 27 (Greek)
10.9 *King James Bible* (Titus 3:5)
10.10 Strong, James. *Strong's Exhaustive Concordance of the Bible.*
© 1890 James Strong, Madison, NJ p. 27 (Greek)
10.11 Donovan, Colin B., retrieved 5/17
https://www.ewtn.com/expert/answers/mortal_versus_v
enial.htm
10.12 Donovan, Colin B., retrieved 5/17
https://www.ewtn.com/expert/answers/mortal_versus_v
enial.htm
10.13 Etymology Online, retrieved 5/17
http://www.etymonline.com/index.php?term=Repent
10.14 retrieved 5/17
http://www.aboutcatholics.com/beliefs/mortal-
sins/
10.15 Donovan, Colin B., retrieved 5/17
https://www.ewtn.com/expert/answers/mortal_
versus_venial.htm
10.16 *King James Bible* (1 Corinthians 6:9-10)
10.17 *King James Bible* (1 Corinthians 6:11)
10.18 Fox News retrieved 5/17
http://www.foxnews.com/story/2008/03/11/ vatican-
adds-seven-new-deadly-sins-including-damaging-
environment-and-drug.html
10.19 *King James Bible* (1 Timothy 6::10)
10.20 *King James Bible* (Ecclesiastes 10:19)
10:21 *King James Bible* (Deuteronomy 28:2)
10.22 *King James Bible* (Matthew 25:40)
10.23 *King James Bible* (2 Thessalonians 3:10-12)

Chapter 12

12.1 Fox News retrieved 5/17
http://www.foxnews.com/story/2009/12/16/rewriti
ng-our-history-changing-our-traditions.html

12.2 Santayana, George, retrieved 5/17
http://thinkexist.com/quotation/those_who_do_n
ot_learn_from_history_are_doomed_to/170710.htm
l

12.3 *King James Bible* (Proverbs 26:4-5)

Glossary

G1 Strong, James. *Strong's Exhaustive Concordance of the Bible.* ©
1890 James Strong, Madison, NJ p. 84 (Hebrew)

G2 Strong, James. *Strong's Exhaustive Concordance of the Bible.*
© 1890 James Strong, Madison, NJ p. 23 (Hebrew)

G3 *Holy Bible, Saint Joseph New Catholic Edition.* copyright 1962,
copyright 1957-1949 Catholic Book Publishing Co., N.Y. p15

G4 Strong, James. *Strong's Exhaustive Concordance of the Bible.*
© 1890 James Strong, Madison, NJ p. 24 (Greek)

G5 *Chambers Dictionary of Etymology.* Copyright © 1988 The H.
W. Wilson Company, New York, NY p. 308

G6 http://www.dictionary.com/browse/frabjous?s=

G7 *Chambers Dictionary of Etymology.* Copyright © 1988 The H.
W. Wilson Company, New York, NY p. 422

G8 Walker, J. Bartholomew, Quadrakoff Emma B., *MeekRaker
Beginnings...* © 2016 Quadrakoff Publications Group, LLC,
Wilmington DE

G9 Walker, J. Bartholomew, Quadrakoff Emma B., *MeekRaker
Beginnings...* © 2016 Quadrakoff Publications Group, LLC,
Wilmington DE p. 7

Other Fine QPG Publications:

MEEKRAKER BEGINNINGS. . .

WISDOM ESSENTIALS—THE PENTALOGY

DONALD TRUMP CANDIDACY
ACCORDING TO MATTHEW?

SHÂMAR TO SHARIA

IT'S NOT JUST A THEORY

CALVARY'S HIDDEN TRUTHS

INEVITABLE BALANCE

OSTIUM AB INFERNO

REINCARNATION —A REASONABLE
INQUIRY

LEARNING HOW TO BE GAY

QPG Publications are available
wherever you buy fine books.

Visit us at MeekRaker.com

www.ingramcontent.com/pod-product-compliance
Lightning Source LLC
Chambersburg PA
CBHW031118020426
42333CB00012B/132